How to use this workbook

Structure

The activities in this workbook will help you to develop the skills and knowledge that you will need to achieve your best grade in A-level English Literature, whichever exam board specification you are following.

Each section offers a clear structure with activities that gradually increase in difficulty:

- **Starting out:** accessible activities that offer an introduction to the topic.
- **Developing your ideas:** skills-building activities that look in more detail at particular aspects of the text.
- **Taking it further:** more challenging tasks that will test your understanding of the text and consolidate your learning.

Boosting your skills

The final chapter of the workbook offers exam-focused activities that allow you to apply the skills you have developed. It also includes step-by-step guidance on the Assessment Objectives, and how to cover them in your written responses.

Features

Key terms

Definitions of key concepts and terminology. Understanding these and using them correctly in your written responses will help you to gain marks for AO1.

Key skills

Concise explanations of important skills to develop during your A-level studies. A variety of skills are covered, from fundamental ones such as analysing the structure of a text or embedding quotations in your writing, up to more advanced skills that are necessary to gain the top grades, such as exploring different interpretations of characters.

Challenge yourself

Advanced tasks that will push you further and help prepare you to achieve your best grade in the exams. They often focus on context (AO3), connections between texts (AO4) or critical interpretations of them (AO5).

Answers can be found at: www.hoddereducation.co.uk/workbookanswers

Introduction: studying *Atonement* at A-level

Your study of novels for Key Stage 3 and GCSE will form a good basis for A-level. However, you will now have to extend your existing skills. In particular, you will need to be more aware of the possible critical approaches to the novel, which is why this workbook devotes a chapter to them. You will also need to consider the novel's social, historical and cultural context, and so one chapter in this workbook focuses on that.

At A-level, too, far more than at GCSE, you need to be aware of how *Atonement* fits into and develops the novel as a genre. This is especially true because McEwan is an extremely well-read author who is well aware of the history of the genre, who makes veiled references to earlier novels in his own text, and who uses the novel to explore the nature of narrative.

Above all, you need to develop your own interpretation of the novel and be able to express this fluently, backing up your arguments with evidence from the text. You will be more fluent if you master the art of using short embedded quotations within your own sentences.

Characters

The study of characters remains important at A-level, but you will be expected to have a deeper awareness of their roles and the dynamics between them. You should avoid falling into the trap of writing about them as if they are real people. They are the author's constructs and should be seen as part of the structure of the novel, and as representing the social and historical context of the novel's settings, as well as the time when the author was writing. This is true of all fiction, but there is an extra layer of construction in *Atonement*, because of the unusual device it uses of portraying one character, Briony, as the author of the whole novel.

Themes and language

Themes remain important, but you will need to show more awareness of how they are reflected in McEwan's language, and be able to demonstrate how his language achieves its effects. There is also the added factor of the different styles in which the four main parts of *Atonement* are written, and how they are appropriate. In writing about these factors, you will need to make correct use of technical terms such as 'metaphor' and 'simile', and terms relating to narrative techniques, such as 'metafiction'.

Gaining an overview

You may read the novel in class, but you should read it to yourself as well – preferably more than once. When you have read the text and understood the plot and the character relationships, you need to develop an overview. Ideally you should be able to remember where major events occur, so that you can find them easily. This will help you when looking for quotations to use as evidence. The 'Plot and structure' section in this workbook will help you to achieve this. An overview will also enable you to analyse the novel's narrative arc.

Using this workbook

You do not necessarily have to attempt all the activities in the workbook: you could pick and choose according to your needs. However, there is a progression within each section, from the basics in 'Starting out' to 'Taking it further'. In addition, 'Challenge yourself' boxes aim to push you that little bit further to help you achieve the top grades. You should also take note of the 'Key skills' and key terms boxes (key terms are highlighted in pink).

Page references are to the Vintage 2002 edition. They will be different if you are reading the book on Kindle, but you will still be able to search for quoted phrases.

AS/A-LEVEL

ENGLISH LITERATURE

WORKBOOK

Atonement

Improve skills • Reinforce understanding • Achieve success

Author and Series Editor: **Steve Eddy**

HODDER
EDUCATION
LEARN MORE

Contents

Plot and structure

A sound knowledge of *Atonement*'s plot is essential in the exam, but you will also need to have an understanding of how its unusual structure works: the overall structure of the 'real' novel, and the separate structure of what is presented as Briony's novel within that whole. This plot device is an example of what is sometimes called **framing**.

Framing: plot device in which a story is presented as part of another story. Another modern novel using framing is Margaret Atwood's *The Handmaid's Tale*.

STARTING OUT

1   Use the table below to identify the characteristics of the four sections of the novel: Parts 1–3 and 'London, 1999' (referred to here as 1999). Tick one box for each characteristic.

CHARACTERISTIC	1	2	3	1999
A 1st person narrative				
B Several characters' narrative perspectives				
C Includes violent attack and physical danger				
D Contains much description of things happening regularly, as opposed to unique events				
E 3rd person but told completely from one character's perspective				
F Reveals 'truth' about other sections				
G Includes details that must have been carefully researched by Briony (and McEwan)				
H Shows how differently an incident can be interpreted				

2   Number these events in order of occurrence (1–8).

EVENT	ORDER
A A wedding	
B A burial	
C Briony is driven to a hotel	
D A vase is broken	
E A pig is caught	
F A play is performed	
G Twins run away	
H Briony tells a young Frenchman she loves him	

3   Which three of these statements are 'true'? Circle the correct statements.

(a) Lola's parents accompany her to the Tallis household.

(b) Pierrot wets the bed.

(c) Briony sees Cecilia in her underwear.

(d) Corporal Nettle plays the piano.

(e) A Stuka plane carries a single thousand-ton bomb.

(f) Briony had an Auntie Aphrodite.

(g) Robbie sees a leg hanging in a tree.

(h) Corporal Mace drowns an airman.

(i) Emily Tallis suffers from migraines.

KEY SKILLS

Commenting on plot

Always bear in mind that the plot works on at least two levels: as Briony's novel and commentary and McEwan's novel, which uses this as a narrative device.

DEVELOPING YOUR IDEAS

4   One widely accepted theory is that most stories follow a five-point design. Make notes below on how this could apply to *Atonement*.

Point 1: The 'initiating incident' that triggers the main action. What is this in *Atonement*? When does it happen? How does it trigger further action? Is there any doubt about what the incident is?

....

....

....

....

....

....

Point 2: Successes and reverses for the main protagonist – Briony. How is she successful at different points in the novel? At what point do things start to go wrong for her? Does it seem as if she will be able to make things right?

....

....

....

....

....

Point 3: Crisis, when there is most at stake for the protagonist. Is there just one crisis, when in theory Briony could still step back from disaster?

....

....

....

....

....

Point 4: Climax – the most dramatically intense moment of the novel. What is this, and what makes it intense? Is there a moment of final suspense involved?

....

....

CONTINUED ➡

Answers can be found at: www.hoddereducation.co.uk/workbookanswers

....

....

....

....

Point 5: Resolution – the restoration of emotional equilibrium, when readers should feel a sense of catharsis. In this novel, this depends on how far Briony has 'atoned'. How far do you think she has made up for her childhood 'crime', and how?

....

....

....

....

....

....

5   Most of the novel's focus is on three periods of time:

- one day in 1935
- a few days in 1940 in Normandy
- about three months (April–July) in London
- one day in 1999.

(a) What are the most obvious parts of the story between 1935 and 1940 that McEwan barely mentions, and that in theory he could have included in a continuous narrative?

....

....

....

....

(b) Imagine you are a going to be interviewing Briony Tallis, now a famous author, in 1999. Write down at least six questions you could ask her about her life to establish how she progressed from her rejection slip from Cyril Connolly (pages 311–15) to becoming a celebrated author in 1999.

....

....

....

....

....

....

CONTINUED

(c) What do you think McEwan achieves by not covering the 'missing' parts of the story from 1935 to 1999?

....

....

....

....

6   In the final section of the novel, we discover that Briony 'made up' the whole of Part 3. Write a paragraph giving your views on why she did not make up a story here in which Robbie and Cecilia forgive her. After all, as the 'author', she could have told any story she wanted.

....

....

....

....

....

....

....

7   How did you feel when you discovered that Briony 'made up' Parts 2 and 3? And how do you feel about this now, looking back on the whole novel? Write a paragraph on this. You might want to use one or more of the words below.

cheated   intrigued   disappointed   impressed   truth   integrity   **postmodern**   clever

....

....

....

....

....

....

....

Postmodern: *Atonement* is postmodern in that it has an unconventional structure and plays with the idea of authorship, persuading us that something is 'true' within the author–reader relationship and then disillusioning us. It also leaves us with several uncertainties.

8   If we follow the conceit of Briony being the author of the novel, what facts are implied about her, and about Lord and Lady Marshall, by the fact that it has now been published?

....

TAKING IT FURTHER

9   Time for some detective work! Suggest how the following shed light on what we eventually discover is the framework of the novel:

(a) Cyril Connolly's comment that a Ming vase is too expensive to take outdoors (page 313).

....

....

....

(b) The colonel writing to Briony and telling her that a Stuka would not have carried a thousand-ton bomb (page 360).

....

....

....

(c) Briony says she has a 'dozen long letters from old Mr Nettle' (page 353).

....

....

....

10 Joe Wright's 2007 film (starring James McAvoy and Keira Knightley) is fairly faithful to the novel, but probably in the interests of fitting a long novel into film format, and because some episodes would be difficult to convey on screen, it omits or only deals very briefly with several of the novel's episodes. Suggest what might be lost by its omission of the following:

(a) Emily Tallis's thoughts while coping with her migraine (Part 1, Chapter 6).

....

....

(b) Most of what happens to Robbie, Mace and Nettle as they join the crowds fleeing on the road to Dunkirk (such as the air attack).

....

....

(c) The scene in Dunkirk when the soldiers come close to seriously harming or even killing an RAF man – who is rescued by Mace.

....

....

(d) The scene when Robbie and Nettle catch a Frenchwoman's pig in Dunkirk.

....

....

(e) Briony's lengthy journey on foot to visit Cecilia.

....

....

CONTINUED ➡

(f) The family reunion and performance of *The Trials of Arabella* in 'London, 1999'.

....

....

11 *Atonement* has been seen as a tragedy. If this is so –

(a) Whose tragedy is it?

....

....

(b) How far do you think there is a tragic inevitability to the novel's events?

....

....

12 Write three paragraphs on how far you agree with this statement:

In *Atonement* McEwan betrays the reader's trust by breaking the implicit agreement that the novel will describe events that are true within the integrity of its own framework.

....

....

....

....

....

....

....

....

....

....

....

....

Challenge yourself

McEwan frequently steps out of the narrative 'present' to give us glimpses of the future, as in the opening of Chapter 13 anticipating Briony's 'crime', or the long passage beginning 'Six decades later' (page 41). What are the effects of this technique?

KEY SKILLS

Commenting on plot

You will earn little credit by simply retelling the story of the novel. Examiners regard this as an indicator of a weak candidate. However, you would earn credit by showing your understanding of how McEwan's unusual framing device works.

Themes

Overview

Remember that themes are the 'big ideas' of a text, which are either deliberately explored by the author or which emerge in the unravelling of the narrative. You may be asked to look at *Atonement* focusing on a particular theme, such as Childhood, but you need to be aware that other themes may well be involved with this theme. For example, childhood would obviously link to Growing up.

STARTING OUT

1   There is no universally accepted list of themes in *Atonement*, but some stand out. Circle the five that you think are most relevant in the list below.

Love and sex	Money and wealth	Parent–child relationships	Misinterpretation
Forgiveness	Social class	Growing up	Atonement
Family	War	Education	Childhood
Innocence and experience	Secrecy	Responsibility	Authorship

2   For each theme that you circled, explain how it could be linked in the novel to one other theme.

(a) ....

....

....

(b) ....

....

....

(c) ....

....

....

(d) ....

....

....

(e) ....

....

....

CONTINUED →

3 (a) Match the line to the theme it most relates to.

LINE	THEME
A He saw it clearly now. The idea was to humiliate him.	Atonement
B It was a leg in a tree.	Justice
C No one in her presence had ever referred to the word's existence.	Misinterpretation
D When their conversation was over, he patted the senior man on the shoulder and seemed to send them on their way.	Innocence and experience
E She knew what was required of her. Not simply a letter, but a new draft ...	Conflict

(b) Explain how each quotation relates to the theme.

A ....

....

B ....

....

C ....

....

D ....

....

E ....

....

4 Comment on how each of the incidents below relates to one or more themes.

(a) Cecilia and Robbie break the vase.

....

....

....

....

(b) Briony tells the police inspector that she saw Robbie with her own eyes.

....

....

....

....

CONTINUED ➡

Answers can be found at: www.hoddereducation.co.uk/workbookanswers

(c) When a major wants Robbie and the corporals to help him 'flush out' some Germans, Nettle refuses, supposedly quoting orders to 'proceed at haste' to Dunkirk, but Robbie has more luck when he tells the major, 'Actually, old boy, to tell the truth, I think we'd rather not.' (page 223).

....

....

....

....

(d) Briony speaks to the young French soldier, who dies holding her hand.

....

....

....

....

(e) Briony's visit to the Imperial War Museum coincides with that of the Marshalls.

....

....

....

....

DEVELOPING YOUR IDEAS

Atonement

5 Atonement is a major theme of the novel. In fact, McEwan's artifice is to present the first three parts of it as Briony's attempt to atone for her 'crime' (page 156) in falsely accusing Robbie.

Consider the word itself. What do you think it means in relation to the novel? Note down your ideas. You could consider:

- What is the significance of 'at-one-ment'?
- How does it relate to forgiveness?
- Can you atone for a crime even after the people you have wronged are dead?

....

....

....

....

....

....

CONTINUED ➡

6   Briony eventually takes on complete responsibility for what she has done to Robbie and Cecilia. But is she right to do this? Can a 13-year-old really be held responsible for a 'crime' in this way? In what ways were others partly to blame?

On a separate sheet of paper, make notes, a spider diagram or a concept map showing:

(a) the case against her

(b) the case in her defence.

Back up your ideas with references to the text where possible.

7   Suggest how the following quotations contribute to the development of the theme:

QUOTATION	HOW IT DEVELOPS THE THEME
A He would never forgive her. That was the lasting damage. (page 234)	....
B You couldn't carry us across the field. You carried the twins, but not us, no. No, you are not guilty. No. (page 263)	....
C Her sister's confirmation of her crime was terrible to hear. (page 336)	....
D 'I'm very very sorry. I've caused you such terrible distress.' (page 348)	....
E She knew what was required of her. Not simply a letter, but a new draft, an atonement, and she was ready to begin. (page 349)	....

CONTINUED

QUOTATION	HOW IT DEVELOPS THE THEME
F Perhaps he's spent a lifetime making amends. (page 357)	....

8   How successful do you feel Briony is in atoning for what she did to Robbie and Cecilia by the end of the novel? Consider:

- Did it help that she gave up a place at Cambridge University to become a nurse?
- How much good do her intentions and feelings of remorse do once Robbie and Cecilia are dead?
- Can atonement take place without forgiveness?
- How far could writing a novel atone for a past crime?
- How meaningful do you find Briony's efforts to give Robbie and Cecilia a fictional happy reunion in Part 3?

Explain your ideas.

....

....

....

....

....

....

....

....

....

....

9   (a) What in your view is the significance of the fact that Briony is revealed to be suffering from vascular dementia in 'London, 1999', and can be expected gradually to lose her mind, even forgetting her 'crime'.

....

....

....

(b) How does this affect how you feel about Briony and what she has done?

....

....

....

CONTINUED ➡

Justice

10 Most people have a concept of justice, and a belief in it being a civilised virtue. It seems fundamental to human understanding, as perhaps shown by the fact that even three-year-olds are quick to say, 'It's not fair!' when they feel mistreated. It is also related to atonement: criminals are said to 'atone' for their crimes by submitting to punishment.

Despite this, justice is difficult to define. It is easier to find examples of justice being done, or of injustice. Use the table below to comment on examples of injustice in *Atonement* and what causes them. Try to think beyond the obvious causes.

INJUSTICE	CAUSES
A Robbie imprisoned	
B The Marshalls getting away with their deception and being highly regarded in society	
C The RAF man being attacked at Dunkirk	

11 Briony, in her 'fictional' Part 3, talks about her hopes that she can get Robbie's false verdict overturned. Cecilia has already said that this is impossible because the case has been shelved and Briony is an 'unreliable witness'.

What is your response to this, given that Briony, as author, could make up any story she wants to here? How does this apparent impossibility of justice contribute to the overall impact of the novel?

12 In *Atonement* how does the theme of justice relate to the following themes? Write your answer on the next page.

(a) social class

(b) money and wealth

(c) growing up

(d) misinterpretation.

CONTINUED ➡

Answers can be found at: www.hoddereducation.co.uk/workbookanswers

....

....

....

....

....

Misinterpretation

13 The conceit of the whole novel is one of misinterpretation: we read assuming that this is a conventional narrative in which what happens is 'true' within the world of the story – then in 'London, 1999' we discover that we have misinterpreted everything we have read so far.

Even within this framework there are many examples of misinterpretation. Complete this table to show who misinterprets and how.

APPARENT EVIDENCE	WHO	HOW
A Robbie enters house barefoot		
B Cecilia's stripping to her underwear at the fountain		
C Figure leaving Lola in the park		
D Frenchmen with 'something in their hands'		
E Robbie's accent and style of speech when asked to 'flush out' some Germans		
F Absence of RAF planes over Dunkirk		

CONTINUED ➡

14 Which of the following are factors that help to explain why Briony is particularly prone to misinterpreting things? Tick the factors you think are applicable.

(a) a lack of intelligence ☐

(b) her imagination ☐

(c) her gender ☐

(d) carelessness ☐

(e) her thirst for explanations. ☐

15 Carefully read the paragraph in Part 1, Chapter 10, page 123 beginning 'At first, when she pushed ...'. Analyse the separate elements that go to make up Briony's misinterpretation of what she sees.

....

....

....

....

....

....

....

16 Fill in the blanks with appropriate words from the list underneath to complete this paragraph on how the theme of misinterpretation appears in the final chapter of Part 1, page 182, in the paragraph beginning 'At first they saw nothing ...':

We are drawn into the collective .... of everyone waiting outside the

Tallis house as they see a shape .... from the mist that appears to be

a giant 'seven or eight feet high'. .... Betty even crosses herself as if

something .... is approaching. The 'apparition' is seen as being 'as

.... as it was purposeful', ... the attitude that is

taken towards Robbie by the family, the police and the .... system:

that he is a .... of sexual ....

| superstitious | inhuman | emerging | legal | anticipating |

| depravity | monster | demonic | delusion |

CONTINUED ➡

Innocence and experience

17 The word 'innocence' can be interpreted in a number of ways in *Atonement*.

Add to the spider diagram below to explore how different ideas about innocence might relate to the following:

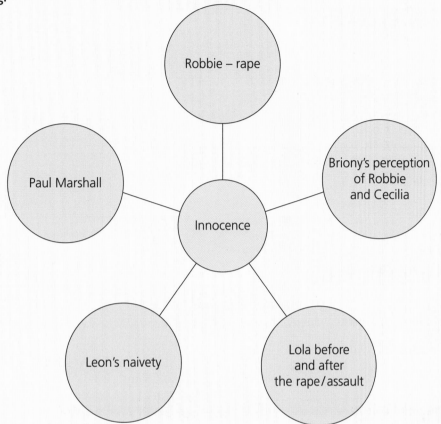

18 Before being accused, Robbie is innocently looking forward to the rest of his life. He has a first-class degree, has suddenly realised he is in love, and plans to become a doctor. Write a paragraph explaining how his experience after this changes his outlook on life and humanity – insofar as we can rely on Briony's account of him.

CONTINUED

19 How do the following quotations develop the theme of innocence and experience in *Atonement*?

QUOTATION	HOW IT DEVELOPS THE THEME
A In the aisles of country churches ... [Briony's] heroines and heroes reached their innocent climaxes and needed to go no further. (page 9)	
B A tall nettle ... its middle leaves turned outwards like hands protesting innocence – this was Lola ... (pages 73–4)	
C Some said that it was innocence, or ignorance of the world, that protected Robbie from being harmed by it ... (page 86)	
D To be cleared would be a pure state. (page 228)	
E It seemed a far-off, innocent time, but it was no more than ten days ago. (page 328)	

Conflict

20 Conflict exists in the novel whenever individuals want opposing things, as well as on the much bigger scale of war, and even at the level of social class.

(a) What physical signs of conflict does Lola falsely blame on the twins, and who is really to blame?

....

....

....

CONTINUED ➡

(b) What is the immediate result of the conflict between Robbie and Cecilia at the fountain, and what might it symbolise?

....

....

....

(c) Name three examples of conflict in *Atonement* involving British soldiers apart from the obvious one of the war with Germany.

....

....

....

....

....

21 How is the experience of Briony and other nurses in the hospital similar to that of the soldiers in the war, and what are the essential differences?

....

....

....

....

KEY SKILLS

Embedding quotations

It is effective to embed quotations in your exam response, making them part of your sentence. Select what you quote so that your sentence works grammatically. For example: 'Robbie believes that to have his name cleared would be to place him in "a pure state", as if he has been cleansed of all guilt, even that of being involved in the war.'

TAKING IT FURTHER

22 Now that you have worked on all the themes, this activity will help you to see how they connect. In the table below, explain how each incident or episode relates to at least two themes.

INCIDENT OR EPISODE	YOUR EXPLANATION
A Grace Turner attacking the police car	....

CONTINUED ➔

INCIDENT OR EPISODE	YOUR EXPLANATION
B Nettle and Mace encouraging Robbie to limp as they pass a sergeant selecting men for 'perimeter defence duties'	
C The cavalry horses being shot on the beach	
D The Marshall wedding	
E The play performance in 'London, 1999'	

23 (a) A further theme, as yet unconsidered in this workbook, is that of friendship. Make notes on how this is explored in the novel. You could consider:

- Leon Tallis and Paul Marshall
- Briony and Lola
- Briony and Fiona (the nurse)
- The corporals and Robbie.

....

....

....

....

....

....

....

CONTINUED ⊙

(b) Now write one or more paragraphs on whichever of these you think is the most significant, explaining why you think this.

....

....

....

....

....

....

....

....

24 Which theme do you think would be seen most differently in the novel by people in the 1930s and 1940s, relative to the modern-day reader? For example, have our ideas about justice changed since then? Explain your ideas.

....

....

....

....

....

....

25 Make notes comparing how the theme of childhood is explored in *Atonement* and one other text that you are studying.

....

....

....

....

....

....

....

....

Challenge yourself

McEwan is an atheist who cannot believe in the original religious sense of atonement: at-one-ment, or reconciliation, with God. How far do you think he nonetheless makes the concept of atonement a meaningful one in this novel?

Characterisation

Character overview

As well as studying individual characters, you will find it helpful to think of the characters in groups. The obvious one is that of the Tallis family, whose complex relationships are explored in Part 1. Closely linked to them are the Quinceys – Briony's cousins and their parents (who do not appear but are described). Robbie is almost part of the Tallis family but is excluded from it – except by Cecilia – when he is accused of assaulting Lola. He becomes, however, part of the small group consisting of him and the two corporals.

KEY SKILLS

Remaining aware of the author

Remain aware of the fact that all the characters in *Atonement* are McEwan's creations: never write about them as if they were real. However, there is a further dimension: the whole novel is conceived as being the work of Briony Tallis, so all the other characters are in a sense her creations too, and are filtered through her character.

STARTING OUT

1   Test your overall knowledge of the characters with this quiz. Which character does each of the following?

(a) sends the wrong letter

(b) wets the bed

(c) rips up a poster

(d) gets a third-class degree

(e) shows ability with a map and compass

(f) saves an airman from being beaten or killed

(g) insists on blankets being correctly folded

(h) thinks Briony is his fiancée

(i) had a husband called Thierry

(j) makes a fortune through confectionery

(k) still wears high heels when nearly 80

(l) has vascular dementia

2   Complete these statements by circling the correct word:

(a) Emily Tallis suffers from (indigestion / migraines / amnesia / septicaemia).

(b) Robbie hopes to become a (lecturer / architect / doctor / gardener).

(c) The main character in Briony's play is (Esmerelda / Amelia / Hermione / Arabella).

(d) Briony insists to the Inspector that she (heard / chased / saw / sensed) Lola's attacker.

(e) Cecilia finds Paul Marshall (boring / interesting / frightening / enigmatic).

(f) The corporals tease Robbie about wanting to get home for (women / food / beer / safety).

(g) In Dunkirk, Nettle finds Robbie somewhere safe to (hide / sleep / drink / pray).

CONTINUED →

Answers can be found at: www.hoddereducation.co.uk/workbookanswers

(h) Briony fails to speak out at her cousin's (party / trial / funeral / wedding).

(i) When Briony visits Cecilia, Robbie (forgives / accuses / hits / ignores) her.

(j) Briony thinks that the night when she helps to treat a badly burned soldier taught her all she understood about (nursing / life / suffering / war).

(k) Briony has done widespread research to write her novel, for example, into what weight of bomb is carried by a (Spitfire / Messerschmitt / Stuka / Lancaster) aircraft.

(l) The elderly Briony (hates / enjoys / resents / mourns) the performance of her play.

3   Complete this Tallis–Quincey family tree.

```
        Henry Tallis                              Quinceys
     ┌───────┴───────┐                       ┌───────┴───────┐
   Clem                           =        Hermione =
              ┌────────┴────────┐     ┌────────┴────────┐
            Leon                                      Pierrot
```

DEVELOPING YOUR IDEAS

4   How would you describe the Tallis family as a whole? Consider:
- their class and social position
- their shared family values
- how supportive or dysfunctional they are.

Write a paragraph about the family and how, as a whole, it affects the narrative.

....

....

....

....

....

....

....

....

....

CONTINUED ⊙

5   Complete the table to suggest how each of these characters is an outsider, and what the effect of this is on other characters, and the plot.

CHARACTER	HOW AN OUTSIDER	EFFECT
Robbie		
Paul Marshall		
Lola		
Senior Inspector		

TAKING IT FURTHER

6   One way to view the characters is to compare them, and even to see them as being deliberately constructed to contrast with each other.

What differences and similarities can you find in these pairings?

(a) Paul Marshall and Robbie Turner

(b) Briony and Lola as teenagers

   CONTINUED ➡

(c) Leon and Cecilia

....

....

....

....

Briony Tallis

As noted above, McEwan presents Briony as the author of the whole novel, which makes her the most important character. It also means that we get some insight into her, not only from how she portrays herself but also through how she portrays other characters.

Another important factor is that we see Briony at three different ages, but with big gaps in between. We can therefore comment on how she has changed.

STARTING OUT

1   Circle the words below that you think apply to 13-year-old Briony.

relaxed	ambitious	imaginative	attention-seeking	judgemental	passionate
objective	sympathetic	lazy	mature	self-assured	affectionate
decisive	deluded	tidy-minded	frustrated	generous	forgiving
rebellious	self-important	determined	self-righteous	broad-minded	

2   How has the 18-year-old Briony changed, and what evidence is there of this?

....

....

....

....

3   What is Briony's response to Cyril Connolly's rejection letter, and what does this show about her character?

....

....

4   How does Part 2 of the novel reveal Briony's character, even though she barely features in it herself?

....

....

....

CONTINUED ➡

5   Which of the following statements about the elderly Briony are true? Circle the correct statements.

(a) She remained unmarried because of her guilt.

(b) She has become more careful.

(c) She has begun to suffer from vascular dementia.

(d) She is conscientious about her responsibilities.

(e) She never managed to become a novelist.

(f) She accepts that her novel of 'atonement' will not be published in her lifetime.

DEVELOPING YOUR IDEAS

6   As the central character and narrator, Briony is bound up with all the main themes of the novel. Suggest at least one way in which she is connected to each theme in the table below.

THEME	CONNECTION
Atonement	
Justice	
Misinterpretation	
Innocence and experience	
Conflict	

CONTINUED

Answers can be found at: www.hoddereducation.co.uk/workbookanswers

7   Look back at the character traits that you circled in Activity 1. Add the five that you think most apply to
    Briony to the spider diagram below. Then add at least one piece of evidence for each trait in the form of:

    • short quotations
    • lines that Briony speaks
    • things that she does.

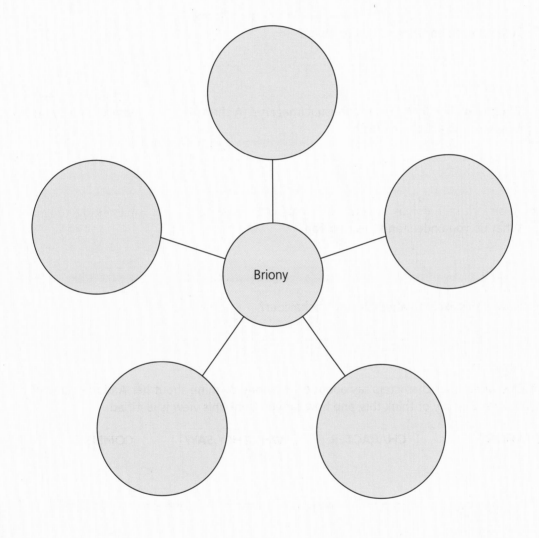

CONTINUED ➡

8   Read the quotations below describing Briony. In a sense they represent the adult Briony's assessments of her 13-year-old self. Answer the questions about each one.

(a) 'She was one of those children possessed by a desire to have the world just so.' (page 4)
   (i) What do you understand this to mean?

   ....

   ....

   (ii) What could be implied by the wording 'possessed by a desire', as opposed to 'who desires'?

   ....

   ....

   ....

(b) 'Briony's [room] was a shrine to her controlling demon.' (page 5)
   (i) What do you understand this to mean?

   ....

   ....

   (ii) What is implied by McEwan's unusual imagery? (A shrine is a holy place visited by devotees of a religion as an act of worship.)

   ....

   ....

(c) 'Her wish for a harmonious, organised world denied her the reckless possibilities of wrongdoing.' (page 5)
   (i) What do you understand this to mean?

   ....

   ....

   (ii) How is this likely to affect Briony's behaviour?

   ....

   ....

9   Read below what other characters say about or to Briony, or think about her. Add the name of the character, why they say or think this, and how far you think this view is justified.

QUOTATION	CHARACTER	WHY THEY SAY/ THINK	COMMENT
A Poor darling Briony, the softest little thing, doing her all to entertain her hardbitten wiry cousins with the play she had written from her heart. (page 65)	....	....	....

CONTINUED ➡

QUOTATION	CHARACTER	WHY THEY SAY/ THINK	COMMENT
B 'There, you see ... Briony's hot-headed decision.' (page 130)			
C 'You really are a tiresome little prima donna.' (page 140)			
D But she's such a fantasist, as we know to our cost. (page 212)			
E Not every child is so purposeful and malign, so consistent over time, never wavering, never doubted. (pages 228–9)			

TAKING IT FURTHER

10 Look back at your answers to Activities 7 and 8. Then, on a separate sheet of paper, use them to plan and write an exam response to the following question:

Discuss the view that the 13-year-old Briony's character and situation make it inevitable that she will commit her 'crime', given the events leading up to it.

Challenge yourself

It could be argued that the adult Briony's attempt to atone for her actions by writing a novel in which she creates a happier outcome for Robbie and Cecilia is both an outrageous act of self-importance and an attempt to let herself off the hook. What are your views on this?

Cecilia Tallis

STARTING OUT

1   Find evidence in the form of quotations or references to the text to support these statements about Cecilia.

(a) She is quite snobbish.

....

....

(b) She is lazy and disorganised.

....

....

(c) She is unconventional.

....

....

(d) She can be kind and sympathetic.

....

....

(e) She can be bad-tempered and irritable.

....

....

(f) She is capable of taking charge and organising things.

....

....

(g) She is brave and loyal.

....

....

2   In Part 1, what is Cecilia's attitude towards the following characters?

(a) Leon

....

(b) Briony

....

CONTINUED ➡

(c) Emily

....

(d) Robbie (before his letter)

....

DEVELOPING YOUR IDEAS

3   Read the letter that Cecilia writes to Robbie (pages 211–13). Summarise the letter and what it reveals about Cecilia's character.

....

....

....

....

....

....

....

....

....

....

....

....

4   We know that Briony's visit to Cecilia in Part 3 is 'fictional', within the framework of the whole novel: it is made up by the adult Briony to give the lovers Cecilia and Robbie a happier ending than they had in 'reality'. But how far do you think Briony is accurate in her portrayal of Cecilia's likely behaviour during this visit?

Write one or more paragraphs explaining your ideas.

....

....

....

....

....

....

....

....

....

....

....

CONTINUED ➡

5   Cecilia is remarkably loyal to Robbie.

   (a) How plausible do you find her continued loyalty, given her family situation, and the context of the 1930–40s? Explain your view.

   ....

   ....

   ....

   ....

   ....

   (b) How do you feel about her loyalty? Is it admirable, or foolishly self-sacrificing and unrealistic?

   ....

   ....

   ....

   ....

   ....

TAKING IT FURTHER

6   Write one or more paragraphs about how Cecilia behaves in Parts 1 and 3 in the context of the era. How does she challenge or conform to feminine conventions of the time?

....

....

....

....

....

....

....

....

....

....

....

....

....

Robbie Turner

Robbie is in an unusual and ambiguous situation. He is both part of the Tallis family in that he lives on their estate and his education has been paid for by Jack Tallis, and yet an outsider in that he is actually the son of their servant Grace. This could be seen as explaining a lot about his character. It also makes him socially interesting.

STARTING OUT

1   Circle the correct words:

Robbie lives on the Tallis estate with his (sister / mother / parents / brother). He went to (Oxford / Cambridge / Bristol / Canterbury) University, where he studied (French / Geography / Politics / English). Although at the start of the novel he is doing some (gardening / brick-laying / bee-keeping / roofing) on the estate, like his (brother / mother / benefactor / father), he wants to become a (soldier / plumber / doctor / poet). He thinks that Cecilia (resents / admires / denies / ridicules) the fact that her father paid for his education. When he types his apology to her he has a book on (literature / anatomy / Communism / Freud) open on his table. He realises that he is in (trouble / bed / competition / love) with her. It is Robbie who (finds / punishes / loses / loathes) the twins, but he is treated as a (hero / stalker / monster / nonentity). He is a good man, as shown by his attempt to (convert / save / entertain / find) the Flemish woman and her son, but he still finds it impossible to (love / save / forgive / forget) Briony.

2   Write what you think these characters might say about Robbie if asked to sum him up at these times.

(a) Jack Tallis at the start of the novel.

....

....

(b) Cecilia just after the fountain incident.

....

....

(c) Briony when she is interviewed by the police.

....

....

(d) Corporal Nettle at the end of Part 2.

....

....

DEVELOPING YOUR IDEAS

3   Write a paragraph in support of this argument:

Robbie may be innocent of the crime of which he is accused, but he is at least partly responsible for what happens to him.

....

....

....

....

....

....

....

4   Now write a paragraph in support of this argument:

Robbie is a completely innocent victim, scapegoated because of his class background and his daring to step outside it.

....

....

....

....

....

....

....

5   What are your real views on the question of Robbie's innocence or guilt? Bear in mind the role that McEwan has him play in the novel.

....

....

....

....

....

....

....

....

CONTINUED ➡

Answers can be found at: www.hoddereducation.co.uk/workbookanswers

6   'By his failure to forgive Briony, a vulnerable child, Robbie shows that he is not worthy of the reader's forgiveness.' How far do you agree or disagree with this view? Explain your ideas.

....

....

....

....

....

....

TAKING IT FURTHER

7   Write at least one paragraph comparing Robbie at the start of Part 1 with the character that he has become at the end of Part 2. How has he developed, and how does McEwan show this?

....

....

....

....

....

....

....

....

....

Challenge yourself

A Marxist critique of the character of Robbie might focus on how he represents the exploitation and victimisation of the working classes by the ruling elite, and their determination to prevent social mobility. How far do you think this view would be valid?

Leon Tallis

Leon, despite his name meaning 'Lionlike', is a rather passive and naïve character, with little ambition or initiative. However, he plays an important role in bringing Paul Marshall into the Tallis household. He also assumes the role of 'man of the house' in the absence of his father and takes charge after Lola has been assaulted. In addition, Briony adores him and wants to stage her play to entertain and impress him.

STARTING OUT

1   Read the section of the novel in which Emily Tallis thinks about her children and focuses on Leon: from 'Shrinking ...' to '... unhappiness and ambition' (page 64).

(a) What is Leon's apparent attitude to his career?

....

....

(b) What prevents Emily from being 'angrier' with Leon about his attitude?

....

....

(c) How does Emily sum up the reasons for Leon's lack of ambition?

....

2   Read the longer passage focusing on Leon as seen from Cecilia's perspective, from 'In Leon's life ...' (last paragraph on page 107) to the end of the first paragraph on page 109 ('... lively spirits'). Then answer the questions below.

(a) What do the opening two sentences tell us about Leon?

....

....

(b) What possible reasons are there in the next three sentences (beginning 'He remembered ...') for Leon being popular?

....

....

(c) How does the account of Leon on page 107 relate to his friendship with Paul Marshall and his bringing Marshall to stay with the family?

....

....

(d) What is meant by 'his equanimity was bottomless'?

....

....

(e) What do you deduce from the phrases that are, by implication, quoted from Leon's conversation – 'a good egg', 'a decent sort', 'jolly happy', 'a licence to print money', 'a brave old stick'?

....

....

(f) What effect does Leon's conversation have on Cecilia?

....

....

....

DEVELOPING YOUR IDEAS

3   How is another side to Leon revealed in the final paragraph of Chapter 13 (page 172) and paragraphs 4–5 of the next chapter (pages 174–5)?

....

....

....

....

4   Given Leon's character as revealed in Activity 2, what might you expect his attitude to be when the crisis of Lola's attack arises and Robbie is accused?

....

....

....

....

TAKING IT FURTHER

5   Suggest why McEwan never tells the story, or presents any other character, from Leon's perspective.

....

....

6   A critic has written:

> Bland and lacking in any kind of insight, Leon is superfluous to the novel. He serves no purpose, and it is hard to see why McEwan has taken the trouble to portray him as a character.

Write at least one paragraph exploring this view and explaining how far you agree or disagree with it.

....

....

....

....

....

....

....

....

....

....

Emily Tallis

Emily features mostly in Chapter 6, in which her family are described from her perspective. She is a loving mother, but is often rendered incapable of taking any active part in the running of the household by her crippling migraines. She puts up stoically with the inattention and frequent absence of her husband Jack. However, she disapproves of him financing Robbie's education.

STARTING OUT

1 Reread Chapter 6 (page 63) and fill in the evidence for the points made in the table below. The first one has been done for you.

POINT	EVIDENCE
A She dreads the pain of her migraines.	She is 'retreating before its threat' (page 63); she is 'rigidly apprehensive, held at knife-point' (page 64).
B She is critical of Cecilia.	
C She is far from being a feminist.	
D She is aware of what goes on in the house, even while suffering from a migraine.	
E She disapproves of her sister Hermione.	

DEVELOPING YOUR IDEAS

2   Bear in mind that Emily may be an **unreliable narrator** and she may misinterpret the evidence around her. (And what we read is what Briony imagines Emily's account might be.) In addition, Emily presents herself as a victim of her migraines who would like to be more involved in her family but is unable to be.

(a) What evidence is there of her misinterpretation – for example, with Paul Marshall?

....

....

(b) What evidence is there of her making bad domestic decisions, both in Chapter 6 and when the twins run away?

....

....

(c) How do you interpret the language, including imagery, with which Emily's migraines are described in the opening paragraph of Chapter 6? What might it reveal about her?

....

....

....

....

(d) How far do you think Emily's self-image is open to question?

....

....

....

....

Unreliable narrator: a character narrating a story who cannot be relied on to give an objective account.

TAKING IT FURTHER

3   Consider this quotation:

> Whenever Mrs Tallis exercised authority in the absence of her husband, the children felt obliged to protect her from seeming ineffectual.
>
> (pages 127–8)

Bearing in mind this quotation, and all the other information you have about Emily, how far do you think McEwan presents her as an effective mother? Write at least one paragraph, considering points on both sides.

....

....

....

....

CONTINUED ➡

....
....
....
....
....

Lola and the twins

Lola Quincey and her younger brothers Jackson and Pierrot are Briony's cousins. They are staying with the Tallises because their mother, Emily's sister Hermione, is having 'a nervous breakdown' – which in reality is an affair with a man in Paris. Lola is 15, so she thinks of herself as an adult, in some ways is close to being one, and has the manipulative skills to get the better of Briony. She is central to the narrative in that she is assaulted by Paul Marshall. Her brothers are unhappy little boys who want to go home. Their most important role in the story is deciding to run away, which necessitates a search for them in the grounds of the house, during which the assault takes place.

STARTING OUT

1 Which of these statements about Lola are true? Circle each correct statement.
(a) Though 15, she still dresses like a little girl.
(b) She threatens to hit the twins.
(c) She is keen to be in Briony's play.
(d) She manipulates Briony into giving her the lead role in the play.
(e) She resists the idea that her parents are getting a divorce.
(f) She tells Paul Marshall off for talking about her parents in front of the twins.
(g) She does not care what Paul Marshall thinks of her.
(h) The twins attack her.
(i) She identifies her rapist to the police.
(j) She marries her rapist.

2 Complete this paragraph about the twins by circling the correct words.

The twins, Jackson and (Perrault / Pierrot / Perrier / Pierre) are only distinguishable

because one has a small triangle missing from his (ear / nose / finger / arm) because he

(patted / chased / cuddled / taunted) a dog. They both say they (hate / love / write / read)

plays, and Pierrot claims that (Briony / Shaw / Arabella / Shakespeare) was just showing

off. Jackson cries because he only has one (ear / sock / shoe / line). Cecilia finds that the

twins' room is very (hot / tidy / cold / messy). When she helps them, they are (proud /

ashamed / grateful / sulky). Jackson wets the bed and is made to wash his own (socks /

face / mattress / sheets). According to their (note / sister / aunt / message) they run

away because Lola and (Betty / Paul / Leon / Cecilia) are horrid to them.

DEVELOPING YOUR IDEAS

3   Read this extract from a student essay on Lola. Add supporting evidence in the form of textual references or quotations in the gaps provided. Use whatever wording is necessary to make the paragraph flow well, such as 'as shown by ...'.

Lola, even more than Briony, is poised between childhood and adulthood. This is revealed by the way she dresses ...

....

....

....

....

....

....

Similarly, she tells Marshall off for speaking about her parents ...

....

....

....

....

....

Emily expects that Lola will be manipulative like her mother, and this proves to be true ...

....

....

....

....

She could also be said to be flirting with Paul Marshall, or at least trying to impress him ...

....

....

....

....

After the assault, Lola seems to retreat into the role of helpless victim ...

....

....

....

....

CONTINUED →

For 18-year-old Briony, Lola's complicity in the crime of perjury is confirmed when ...

....

....

....

....

Our final view of Lola, aged almost 80, is of a vigorous woman who has survived and flourished ...

....

....

....

....

TAKING IT FURTHER

4   Explain:
   - why Lola's role in the novel is sensitive and controversial
   - how a modern audience might see it differently from the way a court might have seen her role as a victim in 1935
   - what your own view of Lola is, and why.

....

....

....

....

....

....

....

Challenge yourself

Lola's name is close to that of Lolita, a 12-year-old girl in Vladimir Nabokov's famously controversial novel of the same name. This first-person narrative presents Lolita as, to some extent, behaving flirtatiously towards her mother's lodger, who becomes sexually obsessed with her. Do you think McEwan could have wanted to imply any connection between Lola and Lolita?

Paul Marshall

Paul Marshall is an ambiguous figure, a self-important bore who boasts about how rich he is becoming with his chocolate bars, yet with more than a hint of sexual menace.

STARTING OUT

1   Marshall is only ever described through the eyes of others: the story is never narrated from his perspective. From a practical narrative point of view, why do you think this is?

....

....

....

....

....

....

2   Which of the following words and phrases are *not* used to describe Marshall? Circle the incorrect descriptions.

(a) nearly handsome

(b) startlingly handsome

(c) hugely rich

(d) across his brow a constellation of acne had a new-minted look

(e) unfathomably stupid

(f) pubic hair growing from his ears

(g) features scrunched up around the eyebrows

(h) his appearance was absurd

(i) his lips had become elongated and innocently cruel

(j) the cruelly handsome plutocrat

3   Cecilia is unimpressed by Marshall, and even finds him ridiculous, but Lola finds that contrasting aspects of him form 'an attractive combination'. What are these aspects?

....

....

DEVELOPING YOUR IDEAS

4   Read the last part of Chapter 5, from 'The tall man in a white suit ...' (page 58) to the end.

(a) In what ways could it be argued that Marshall tries to make Lola like him?

....

....

....

....

....

....

CONTINUED ➔

(b) What evidence is there that Lola does like him?

....

....

....

....

(c) How do both Lola and Marshall demonstrate dishonesty, and what might this shared moment anticipate in the plot?

....

....

....

....

5 Read Chapter 11 from 'All eyes were on Lola' to '"I suppose they've been through a lot lately"' (pages 141–2). How is Marshall's character and his relationship with Lola demonstrated here?

....

....

....

....

....

TAKING IT FURTHER

6 Write at least one paragraph explaining how McEwan presents Marshall in an ambiguous way and what he achieves by doing so.

....

....

....

....

....

....

....

....

....

Challenge yourself

In terms of symbolism and ideas about social class, how do you interpret the fact that Marshall is hoping to get rich by selling Amo bars to the army? You could think about how a Marxist critic might see him.

Corporals Nettle and Mace

Nettle and Mace are the two Cockney corporals who make their way to Dunkirk with Robbie in Part 2. They rely on his navigational skills and knowledge of French, but they also help him in other ways. We also find out in 'London, 1999' that Nettle's letters have helped the adult Briony to piece together Robbie's story.

STARTING OUT

1   Sort out in your mind which corporal is which by matching them to the descriptions below.

DESCRIPTION	NETTLE	MACE
A Big hands		
B Small, sharp features		
C Plays pub piano		
D Restrains Robbie from attacking a French civilian		
E Helps Robbie catch a pig		
F Rescues an airman		
G Last person Robbie ever speaks to		

2   Now answer these questions:

(a) Which corporal asks why a private like Robbie speaks 'like a toff'?

....

(b) What was Mace's job before the war?

....

(c) What does Nettle praise when he is slightly drunk?

....

(d) What does Nettle think of giving the French brothers in return for food?

....

(e) How do Mace and Nettle get Robbie out of joining the Major in attacking some Germans?

....

....

(f) Who does Robbie think of as a 'brave bear', and why?

....

DEVELOPING YOUR IDEAS

3   How do the corporals and Robbie help each other?

....

....

....

....

....

TAKING IT FURTHER

4   McEwan could have had Robbie finding his way to Dunkirk on his own. What do you think the corporals add to the novel as characters? Think, for example, about:

   ● their class

   ● their qualities

   ● their relationship with Robbie

   ● how they deepen our understanding of Robbie.

....

....

....

....

....

....

....

....

....

....

Challenge yourself

If you know any Shakespeare comedies, how do Nettle and Mace compare with some of the 'commoner' (non-noble) characters in them, such as Sir Toby and Sir Andrew in *Twelfth Night*, Stephano and Trinculo in *The Tempest*, Launcelot Gobbo in *The Merchant of Venice*, or Grumio in *The Taming of the Shrew*? Think, for example, of what they value, their manner, and their attitude towards authority.

Writer's methods: language and style

Commenting effectively on language and style is a relatively high-level skill. However, it is particularly relevant to *Atonement* because its unusual structure involves a variety of styles, depending on the particular narrative viewpoint being adopted.

STARTING OUT

Genre

1 *Atonement* at different times seems to be in the style of several different genres, so that the language varies. Look at the genres in the table below and suggest how and at what points the novel could be said to be in each genre, and how this might influence its style.

GENRE	WHEN AND HOW	INFLUENCE ON STYLE
A Crime/detective (e.g. Agatha Christie)		
B Country House (e.g. Jane Austen)		
C Bildungsroman		

CONTINUED ➡

GENRE	WHEN AND HOW	INFLUENCE ON STYLE
D War		
E Journey		

Bildungsroman: a coming-of-age novel in which a main character or narrator grows up, in the process learning lessons about life that are often difficult and painful, and which often involve moving from naïve innocence to knowledge and even disillusionment. Examples include *To Kill a Mockingbird* (Harper Lee), *The Kite Runner* (Khaled Hosseini), *Jane Eyre* (Charlotte Brontë) and *Anita and Me* (Meera Syal).

Settings

2   Another overall influence on style and language is the range of settings. Setting creates atmosphere, which in turn can prepare us for particular sorts of events.

In the space below, list or visually map what you consider to be the most important settings in the novel, and any key events that take place there.

....

....

....

....

....

....

....

....

....

CONTINUED ➡

Viewpoints

3 Part of the structure of *Atonement* is that the story is at different times told from the viewpoint of different characters. In 'London, 1999' this is in the elderly Briony's first-person narrative; more often, the writing is in the third person. Only occasionally does the writing seem to slip into the omniscient narrator viewpoint.

List the characters from whose viewpoint the story is told at different points.

....

....

> Omniscient narrator: the narrative viewpoint or technique in which the author assumes complete knowledge of all the characters' thoughts and actions, and presents them in an apparently objective way.

4 In the case of Briony and Robbie, how their story is told changes at different stages in their lives. For each of these two characters, identify three stages in their narration, and how each is characterised by a particular perspective.

	STAGE	PERSPECTIVE
BRIONY		
1		
2		
3		
ROBBIE		
1		
2		
3		

CONTINUED ➡

5   Name four relatively important characters who never have the story told from their viewpoint.

....

6 (a)   Write two or three narrative sentences that McEwan might have included if he had decided to tell some of the story from the viewpoint of the senior police inspector.

....

....

(b)   What do you think McEwan gains by never taking us inside the mind of the police inspector?

....

....

....

KEY SKILLS

Using literary terminology

Weave your identification of a technique into the sentence in which you analyse its effect. Example: 'The metaphor in which Emily sees her migraine as a "caged panther" shows that she regards her condition as a dangerous threat, though one that can to some extent be contained.'

Notes and letters

7   List all the notes and letters, quoted or referred to, used to advance the narrative throughout *Atonement*, and make brief notes on how they are used. One has been done for you.

NOTE OR LETTER	HOW THEY ARE USED
Robbie's two letters of apology to Cecilia in Part 1	They reveal Robbie's desire for Cecilia, alongside his ability to write a polite letter. His giving the wrong one to Briony is catastrophic for him, as the letter makes Briony think he is a sex maniac, which heavily influences her interpretation of his later behaviour, and her decision that it must be him who has assaulted Lola.
....	....
....	....
....	....
....	....
....	....

CONTINUED →

Answers can be found at: www.hoddereducation.co.uk/workbookanswers

NOTE OR LETTER	HOW THEY ARE USED
....	....
....	....
....	....
....	....
....	....
....	....
....	....
....	....
....	....
....	....
....	....
....	....
....	....
....	....
....	....
....	....

8 One obvious use of language is in the different styles of speech used by the characters. Find three examples of speech that you think particularly express three different characters. Copy out a sentence and explain what you think the style of speech reveals in each case.

Example A:

....

....

Example B:

....

....

Example C:

....

....

Challenge yourself

Read the quotation from *Northanger Abbey* given before the start of *Atonement*. Then research the plot of this novel and read around the quotation – or read more of the novel. How do you think it relates to *Atonement*?

DEVELOPING YOUR IDEAS

Briony's viewpoint

9 Strictly speaking, even though some of the story in Part 1 is told from the viewpoint of the 13-year-old Briony, it is filtered through the mind of her 18-year-old self, and perhaps even that of the older author who has made an unspecified number of revisions to her original text. Despite this, some of the language might have been chosen by a literary-minded and precocious 13-year-old.

Find two examples of this in the vocabulary of Chapter 1.

....

....

....

10 Reread the passage in Chapter 7 from 'It is hard to slash at nettles ...' (page 73) to '... looked around her' (page 76), taking careful note of how Briony's viewpoint is presented. Then answer the questions below.

(a) The opening sentence is presented as if it states a universal truth, but how, in fact, might it be more subjective?

....

....

....

(b) How does the language of the first paragraph express Briony's feelings about Lola? Find and explain three examples.

....

....

....

....

....

....

....

....

(c) What is conveyed in the phrase 'It was regrettable'?

....

....

CONTINUED ➡

(d) How does Briony (actually McEwan) use language to express her contemptuous dismissal of herself up to this point in the second paragraph? Find at least two examples and comment on them.

....

....

....

(e) How does the next paragraph, beginning 'Soon, it was the action ...' reveal Briony's essentially childish mentality, coupled with a particular tendency to take herself seriously? Comment on at least two examples.

....

....

....

....

(f) How does McEwan use language to signify that the episode is gradually coming to a close in the final paragraph?

....

....

....

....

11 Read the opening paragraph of Part 3 and answer the questions below.

(a) How might the opening two sentences be seen as the writing of the 18-year-old Briony? Analyse the vocabulary, imagery and sentence structure.

....

....

....

....

....

(b) What mood is conveyed by the paragraph as a whole, and how?

....

....

....

....

....

....

CONTINUED ➡

(c) How does the sentence beginning 'The senior staff ...' create a sense of Briony, as a new recruit, being excluded.

....

(d) Why might younger doctors be 'a little taller' and seem 'more aggressive', and what might the consultant be thinking as he gazes across the Thames?

....

....

12 Now compare the passages written from teenage Briony's viewpoint with the opening paragraph of 'London, 1999' (page 353). Write a paragraph on how the viewpoint and tone of the writing have changed. Include short quotations to illustrate your points.

....

....

....

....

....

....

....

....

Robbie's viewpoint

13 (a) Read the opening paragraph of Part 2. How does this compare with the opening of Part 3? Write a paragraph analysing the style.

Consider:

- what details are included
- what insights we get into Robbie's mind
- sentence lengths and types
- vocabulary
- imagery.

....

....

....

....

....

....

....

....

CONTINUED ➡

(b) Explain how the style is appropriate to Robbie's situation.

....

....

....

....

Imagery and symbolism

14 Ian McEwan has said that he likes to use imagery sparingly so that it has more impact. Look at his images below and evaluate their effectiveness. Write sentences embedding the image, or a key part of it, and incorporating the name for the type of image in the sentence.

(a) Cecilia has a 'blossoming need for a cigarette' (page 18)

....

....

(b) 'Did her sister also have a real self concealed behind a breaking wave ...?' (page 36)

....

....

(c) 'the long grass was already stalked by the leonine yellow of high summer' (page 38)

....

....

(d) Emily's 'alert senses [are] fine-tuned like the cat's whiskers of an old wireless' (page 66)

....

....

(e) 'a matching set of sharpened kitchen knives would be drawn across her optic nerve' (page 67)

....

....

(f) Emily sees her household as 'a troubled and sparsely populated continent from whose forested vastness competing elements' demand her attention (page 70)

....

....

(g) The summer evening has 'its heavy fragrance, its burden of pleasures' (page 101)

....

....

(h) 'She was like a bride-to-be who begins to feel her sickening qualms as the day approaches' (page 169)

....

....

CONTINUED ⮞

(i) '… she marched into the labyrinth of her own construction' **(page 170)**

....

....

(j) Robbie sees a view 'like something oriental on a dinner plate' **(page 194)**

....

....

15 Read the first two paragraphs of Chapter 7 (pages 72–3). Find three images used in the description of the temple. Identify what type of image each is (e.g. simile), and its effect. For a long image, you could write the beginning and end, with '…' in between.

Image A: ....

Type of image: ....

Your analysis: ....

....

Image B: ....

Type of image: ....

Your analysis: ....

....

Image C: ....

Type of image: ....

Your analysis: ....

....

16 Some features of the novel could be seen as symbols, though they are relatively open-ended rather than having indisputable meanings. Make notes on your ideas about the possible symbolism of the following:

(a) the vase (pages 22, 29, 333)

....

....

....

(b) the Amo bar (pages 61–2)

....

....

....

CONTINUED ➡

(c) the leg in the tree (page 192)

....

....

....

(d) the sugared almonds (page 256)

....

....

....

17 Paul Marshall and Lola are associated with examples of architecture based on that of ancient classical Greece:

- the rape or assault takes place by the Greek-style temple in the grounds of the Tallis house
- their wedding takes place in a London church that resembles a Greek temple
- the last time Briony sees the couple it is outside the Imperial War Museum, whose architecture resembles the other two buildings, with its neoclassical façade (find pictures online).

(a) What values do you think are associated in British culture with ancient classical Greece and with neoclassical architecture? Research this question if necessary. (Think of philosophers such as Plato and Aristotle.)

....

....

....

....

(b) What do you think McEwan could intend by associating the Marshalls and their conventionally 'successful' marriage with neoclassical architecture?

....

....

....

....

KEY SKILLS

When analysing and evaluating images, look very closely at the exact use of words and at the **connotations** of the image.

Connotations: what a reader would tend to associate with a word or phrase; for example, one might associate 'lion' with courage, danger, wildness, rulership, heat, and so on.

Challenge yourself

What significant differences can you find in the overall style of each section of the novel, and what do you think they add to the novel?

TAKING IT FURTHER

Foreshadowing

18 McEwan often uses the technique of foreshadowing.

    (a) Look up the examples below and make brief notes on their effects. Bear in mind the way in which McEwan makes the reader of the novel aware that it is fictional.

        (i) The last two paragraphs of Chapter 3 (pages 41–2)

....

....

....

        (ii) 'all outcomes, on all scales – from the tiniest to the most colossal – were already in place'
        (page 53)

....

....

....

        (iii) 'In the years to come he would often think back to this time'
        (page 90)

....

....

....

        (iv) 'Within the half hour Briony would commit her crime'
        (page 156)

....

....

....

Foreshadowing: anticipating what is to come later in the novel by referring to it; sometimes called 'temporal prolepsis'.

    (b) Now write a paragraph summarising the effect of the technique throughout the novel. Refer to specific examples where appropriate.

....

....

....

....

....

....

....

CONTINUED ➔

Answers can be found at: www.hoddereducation.co.uk/workbookanswers

....

....

....

Stream of consciousness

19 McEwan often uses stream of consciousness, in fact a particular version of this technique: free indirect style. One famous pioneer of this technique was Virginia Woolf, a novelist who has evidently influenced the teenage Briony.

(a) Read the second paragraph of Part 1, Chapter 6 (pages 64–5), in which Emily is trying to forestall a migraine, and is lying on her bed thinking about her family. Suggest why stream of consciousness is particularly appropriate for Emily. (Hint: it would not work so well for Leon.)

....

....

(b) Write a paragraph about how Emily's character and preoccupations are conveyed using free indirect style. Consider:

- what actually happens in this paragraph
- how the progress of Emily's thoughts is conveyed
- how the language reflects Emily's character and attitudes
- the use of questions and exclamations
- the use of dashes
- the use of minor sentences.

....

....

....

....

....

....

....

....

....

Stream of consciousness: technique attempting to reproduce the inner workings of a character's mind.

Free indirect style: a version of stream of consciousness in which the story is told in the third person, but taking on some of the features of one character's speech and outlook.

Minor sentence: grammatically incomplete sentence – that does not have the grammatical bare minimum of a subject and an active verb.

CONTINUED ➡

(c) The fictionalised Cyril Connolly writes Briony an encouraging and constructive rejection letter (pages 311–15). He suggests that her novella *Two Figures by a Fountain* owes 'a little too much to the techniques of Mrs Woolf' (page 312) and we read that she has read Woolf's experimental novel *The Waves* three times (page 282). Read the opening to Virginia Woolf's novel *Mrs Dalloway*, below, and then, on a separate piece of paper, write a comparison of its style – especially its use of stream of consciousness – with the paragraph of Emily's thoughts referred to above. Bear in mind the bullet points in part (b) of this activity, and how they might apply to *Mrs Dalloway*.

> Mrs Dalloway said she would buy the flowers herself. For Lucy had her work cut out for her. The doors would be taken off their hinges; Rumpelmayer's men were coming. And then, thought Clarissa Dalloway, what a morning – fresh as if issued to children on a beach.
>
> What a lark! What a plunge! For so it had always seemed to her, when, with a little squeak of the hinges, which she could hear now, she had burst open the French windows and plunged at Bourton into the open air. How fresh, how calm, stiller than this of course, the air was in the early morning; like the flap of a wave; the kiss of a wave; chill and sharp and yet (for a girl of eighteen as she then was) solemn, feeling as she did, standing there at the open window, that something awful was about to happen; looking at the flowers, at the trees with the smoke winding off them and the rooks rising, falling; standing and looking until Peter Walsh said, 'Musing among the vegetables?' – was that it? – 'I prefer men to cauliflowers' – was that it? He must have said it at breakfast one morning when she had gone out on to the terrace – Peter Walsh. He would be back from India one of these days, June or July, she forgot which, for his letters were awfully dull; it was his sayings one remembered; his eyes, his pocket-knife, his smile, his grumpiness and, when millions of things had utterly vanished – how strange it was! – a few sayings like this about cabbages.
>
> She stiffened a little on the kerb, waiting for Durtnall's van to pass. A charming woman, Scrope Purvis thought her (knowing her as one does know people who live next door to one in Westminster); a touch of the bird about her, of the jay, blue-green, light, vivacious, though she was over fifty, and grown very white since her illness. There she perched, never seeing him, waiting to cross, very upright.

20 Now read the whole letter from the fictionalised Cyril Connolly. It seems to be a response to an early draft of Briony's novella, which focuses entirely on the scene she saw from a window involving Robbie and Cecilia at the fountain.

(a) How far do you think his comments still apply to the redrafted version of Briony's account? For example, consider his comments on the presentation of the young girl's perspective.

....

....

....

....

....

....

(b) What image does he compliment her on that is retained in the novel, and how is it effective?

....

....

....

CONTINUED ➡

(c) What advice does it appear that Briony acted on, both in Part 1 and Part 2 of the novel? Explain how the novel shows her response to his recommendations.

....

....

....

....

....

....

....

....

21 Read the student comment below and explain how far you agree or disagree with it.

'Atonement' is a very self-conscious work, more about the whole process of writing a novel, and its possible motivation, than about what happens to a particular set of characters. In a sense there is only one character – Briony, and while we might admire McEwan's ability to portray her thought processes at three key stages of her life, the novel is ultimately frustrating and stifling, because McEwan cheats us out of the suspension of disbelief that is essential to enjoying a novel. We discover that we have been in Briony's head all along. For all the virtuoso writing with which individual characters are conveyed, they are all just aspects of Briony. Even Part 2 is just the product of the adult Briony's research. This is not a novel about life; it is a novel about writing a novel.

Your comments:

....

....

....

....

....

....

....

....

Challenge yourself

Find what the fictionalised Cyril Connolly writes to Briony about 'The crystalline present moment' (page 312). How far do you think McEwan achieves what Connolly describes here?

Contexts

You should be aware of the text both as a product of its historical, social and cultural context, and of how readers and critics have interpreted it. As *Atonement* was published in 2002, the broad historical context is fairly close to that of the present day. However, there is also the historical context of the period in which the first three sections of the novel are set to consider: the period leading up to World War II, when people in Britain were uncertain whether there would be a war, and then the war itself – at a point when it seemed that Germany might win. Finally, you need to understand:

- the wider context of the novel as a genre
- the special influence of Jane Austen's *Northanger Abbey* on *Atonement*
- the influence of Virginia Woolf, especially on Part 1
- developments in literary postmodernism.

To gain credit for AO5 you will have to show an awareness of relevant context, incorporating references in your response where appropriate.

> ## KEY SKILLS
>
> Incorporating context
>
> If you answer the question fully then you will be including context without having to make a special effort to add it. You should not add unintegrated references to context as an afterthought.

Historical and social context, 1935–40 and 1999

STARTING OUT

1 What is the social class background of the Tallis family, and how might this be reflected in their house and grounds?

....

....

....

2 Make notes on the likely attitudes of the older generation of the Tallis family (Emily and Jack) to the following, and what evidence there is in the novel:

(a) Sex before marriage

....

....

(b) Marriage and divorce

....

....

(c) Servants

....

....

CONTINUED ➡

(d) The 'lower classes' generally

....

....

(e) Police officers

....

....

(f) Britain

....

....

(g) Education for women

....

....

3 Why are Robbie and the corporals making their way to Dunkirk in Part 2?

....

....

....

4 Which of the following rules are evidence of how strict conditions were for trainee nurses in 1940? Circle the correct statements.

(a) They must fold blankets with the label facing up.

(b) They have to carry ten bedpans the length of the ward.

(c) They must not reveal their first names to patients.

(d) They are addressed only by their numbers.

(e) They must not stand putting their weight on one leg.

(f) They have to march in step when with another trainee.

(g) They have to wear perfectly neat starched collars.

(h) They must leave bed castors (wheels) lined up and facing inwards.

(i) They must not walk down the ward empty-handed.

(j) They are allowed only three cigarettes a day when on duty.

DEVELOPING YOUR IDEAS

5 Read the following account from *The Times* newspaper and answer the questions that follow.

The Defence of Dunkirk, 30 May 1940

The following communiqués were issued by the French High Command today:

The French and British troops that are fighting in Northern France are maintaining with a heroism worthy of their traditions a struggle of exceptional intensity. For a fortnight past they have been fighting a battle separated from the main body of our armies by German formations, which are being constantly reinforced. Although ceaselessly attacked on their two flanks from the east and west, they are disputing every inch of ground to the enemy and clinging to their ground or counter-attacking with as much stubbornness as bravery.

CONTINUED ➔

While they were facing this assault, the ally which, under the direct command of King Leopold III, was defending the positions of the Scheldt and the coast north-east of Ostend received from its King the order to cease fire, thus opening to the enemy the road to Ypres, to Furnes, and to Dunkirk. Since then our troops, under the command of General Blanchard and General Prioux, in close collaboration with the British Army under Lord Gort, have had to face an increased danger.

Showing in these grave circumstances indomitable resolution, they are making every effort to manoeuvre towards the coast at the price of very hard fighting. The French Navy, in defending the ports and lines of communication, is lending them powerful support. Under the command of Admiral Abrial, with a very large number of ships, it is engaged in supplying the fortified camp of Dunkirk and the troops dependent on it, in co-operation with land and naval aircraft, which are perpetually in action.

(a) How does the article reflect McEwan's depiction of events in Part 2 of the novel?

....

....

....

....

....

....

....

(b) How does Lord Gort, mentioned here, feature in Part 2?

....

....

(c) In what notable way does the final paragraph seem at odds with McEwan's account?

....

....

....

....

6   Read the account below from *The Times* and answer the questions that follow.

Waiting to Embark, 5 June 1940

Among the pictures published on another page this morning, one in particular will strike the imagination of everyone who studies it. It is the long, narrow photograph of the beach at Dunkirk, with the troops waiting on it to be embarked. That huge open space, with never a shred of cover; those few and minute boats; those masses of waiting men, practically unable to do anything to defend themselves, waiting, waiting under the actuality or the possibility of murderous attack. How immeasurably long must have seemed those hours of waiting, even to those in front, while to those in the rear every moment must have seemed a year. And these were men already worn out by day after day of the most exacting kind of fighting, carried out under conditions devilishly designed to destroy the nerve as well as the body.

CONTINUED ➡

If ever there was excuse for a panic, surely it was here and on the other similar places where the British Expeditionary Force and the French and Belgian soldiers that came along with them were waiting to be embarked. Yet there they stand, queued up a little raggedly, it is true, but each waiting his proper turn to enter – what? The cinema? The beach negro minstrel enclosure? No, the little boat that, if it is not hit, may transfer him to a larger boat, out of which, if it is not hit, he may be shipped on board a still larger boat which, if it is not hit, may land him on the English coast. Coming at the end of the heroic retreat, this scene puts upon it the crown of military valour and virtue. Not for the first time in history have British troops confounded their enemy by their power to keep still and endure; but never has their steadiness been so tried and so triumphant as here.

(a) McEwan's account does not cover the actual embarkation of soldiers from Dunkirk onto the boats. But how far does McEwan's account seem to fit with the details given here?

....

....

....

....

....

(b) Why do you think McEwan chooses not to include the embarkation, given that it would provide very dramatic material for the novel?

....

....

....

7   Read the accounts below from *The Times* and answer the questions that follow.

Rapid flow of troops through Dunkirk, 1 June 1940

British and French troops are being steadily re-embarked at Dunkirk, and the number already withdrawn has surpassed the most optimistic expectations.

The operation of retreat and embarkation in view of the enemy, the most difficult in warfare, is being carried out with success thanks to the ably co-ordinated action of the three arms of the Allies. The losses, though inevitably heavy in numbers, have been unexpectedly small in proportion to the effectives involved.

RAF bombers have helped in the withdrawal of the British Expeditionary Force by intense bombing of the German lines of communication. There has been a marked decrease in enemy air activity.

Enemy Checked by Floods

British and French naval forces are assisting in covering the withdrawal, and the RAF is still playing its magnificent part.

In this confined area the men of the three Services can see combined operations being carried out under their very eyes. Actually, of course, sea-power and air-power have been helping land-power throughout; but the soldier in the field does not always observe their action, and sometimes does not realise it. When bombs drop near him he wants to see the hostile bomber brought down by a friendly fighter, and can seldom appreciate the fact that but for action taken by aircraft many miles away three times as many bombs might have been dropped in his neighbourhood.

CONTINUED ➡

(a) How do these accounts relate to the experiences of Robbie and the corporals on the way to Dunkirk?

....

....

....

....

(b) How do the accounts seem to relate to the experiences and attitudes of the men who attack the RAF man in Part 2, from 'He must have been short ...' (page 250) to the end of page 253?

....

....

....

....

8   Read the following article from *The Times* and answer the questions that follow. The article begins with a quotation from Shakespeare's *The Merchant of Venice* in which a comic servant gives very misleading directions to his father, who fails to recognise his son.

> **Names Wiped Out, 7 June 1940**
>
> 'Master young gentleman, I pray you which is the way to Master Jew's?'
>
> 'Turn up on your right hand at the next turning, but at the next turning of all on your left; marry at the very next turning, turn of no hand, but turn down indirectly to the Jew's house.'
>
> Launcelot Gobbo's directions to his true-begotten father would make a good model for the right answer to a stranger of ingratiating manner, dressed perhaps as a clergyman or a police inspector, who should ask the way to the Grysdal Ballace or the village of Liddle Vallop. We have been warned by authority that there will be many such dangers ahead, now that signposts and milestones have been taken away or obliterated all over the country; and dangers much greater than the bear that lurks to right or left or the Major Road who truculently orders the motorist to respect his rank. The man who knows where he is and which is the way to Walsingham, or wherever it may be, must be very chary of imparting his knowledge.
>
> Even the indignation aroused by the thought of all the enemy spies and the native fifth columnists, crawling all over the country on their nauseous activities, cannot drive out all enjoyment of the comic side of it – the thought of an honest Briton, for instance, on his lawful business, completely lost and unable to persuade a soul to tell him where he is. But, as a road official has said, it is better that a hundred people should be inconvenienced than that one should be supplied with information that he should not have.

(a) The article imagines spies asking the way to Crystal Palace or the village of Little Wallop. How does their pronunciation contradict what Briony has evidently heard?

....

....

(b) What are 'fifth columnists' and how do they feature in Parts 2 and 3?

....

....

CONTINUED ➡

(c) How do Briony's difficulties connect her to her account of Robbie in Part 2?

....

....

(d) How do her difficulties in finding her way symbolically express her moral and emotional difficulties?

....

....

(e) How does this article provide context for the difficulties Briony experiences in finding her way to her cousin's wedding, as well as contributing to a major motif of the novel? Write a paragraph explaining your ideas, using short quotations from the text.

....

....

....

....

....

....

....

....

TAKING IT FURTHER

9   It could be argued that McEwan wrote *Atonement* at a time when society was taking an increasingly postmodern view of events. Tony Blair was Prime Minister, and his government became known for its manipulation of the truth in what was called 'Spin', and later for the debate over whether Iran had weapons of mass destruction. In what ways can you argue that *Atonement* is a product of this era?

....

....

....

....

....

10 In what ways does McEwan depict Britain as having changed since the war in 'London, 1999'?

....

....

....

....

CONTINUED ➡

11 Write a plan for an essay giving your views on this statement:
    Atonement is as much about social history as it is about individual characters.

    ....

    ....

    ....

    ....

    ....

    ....

    ....

    ....

    ....

    ....

Challenge yourself

Research the evacuation of Dunkirk. How accurate a picture of the situation at Dunkirk do you think McEwan (through Briony) presents, and how important do you think it is for the novel to be historically accurate?

Literary context

Ian McEwan is a well-read author whose work is highly original and yet influenced by authors who have gone before him. At times he even refers to other famous authors and their works, and he prefaces *Atonement* with a significant quotation from *Northanger Abbey*, by Jane Austen (1775–1817). He assumes that at least some of his readers will have read the works referred to and therefore benefit from his use of intertextuality.

Intertextuality: adding implied meaning to a text by referencing other texts.

STARTING OUT

1   What nineteenth- or twentieth-century novels have you read that could be said to form part of the English tradition that has influenced *Atonement*? For example, you may have read one or more of these:
    ● Jane Austen, *Pride and Prejudice*, *Emma* or *Northanger Abbey*
    ● Charlotte Brontë, *Jane Eyre* or *Villette*
    ● Emily Brontë, *Wuthering Heights*
    ● Charles Dickens, *Great Expectations*
    ● George Eliot, *Middlemarch*
    ● EM Forster, *A Passage to India*
    ● LP Hartley, *The Go-Between*

    Focus on three such novels. If you do not know three, research the plots, characters and themes of some of those listed above. Then look back at the Themes chapter in this workbook to remind yourself of some key themes of *Atonement*. On a separate sheet of paper, using Venn diagrams, spider diagrams, bullet lists or some other visual form of representation, find similarities between your chosen three novels and *Atonement*.

CONTINUED ➡

2   In Part 1 of *Atonement* Cecilia is reading Samuel Richardson's novel *Clarissa* (1748). This is an epistolary novel. Letters and notes convey important information in *Atonement*. List other novels you can think of that use letters, and any connections you can find of how their use of letters is similar to that in *Atonement*.

....

....

....

....

....

....

....

....

Epistolary: narrated through the form of letters.

DEVELOPING YOUR IDEAS

3   McEwan has acknowledged Jane Austen's *Northanger Abbey* as an important influence on *Atonement*, and he prefaces his novel with a quotation from Austen's novel. Read these passages from earlier in the novel, and then McEwan's preface, before answering the questions that follow.

Text A:

Catherine Morland is a teenage girl who enjoys reading Gothic novels. She is visiting the home of her new friend, Eleanor Tilney, who is speaking about her mother at the start of this extract. Eleanor's brother is Henry; her father is General Tilney.

> 'She has been dead these nine years.' And nine years, Catherine knew, was a trifle of time, compared with what generally elapsed after the death of an injured wife, before her room was put to rights. 'You were with her, I suppose, to the last?' 'No,' said Miss Tilney, sighing; 'I was unfortunately from home. Her illness was sudden and short; and, before I arrived it was all over.' Catherine's blood ran cold with the horrid suggestions which naturally sprang from these words. Could it be possible? Could Henry's father –? And yet how many were the examples to justify even the blackest suspicions! And, when she saw him in the evening, while she worked with her friend, slowly pacing the drawing-room for an hour together in silent thoughtfulness, with downcast eyes and contracted brow, she felt secure from all possibility of wronging him. It was the air and attitude of a Montoni!* What could more plainly speak the gloomy workings of a mind not wholly dead to every sense of humanity, in its fearful review of past scenes of guilt? Unhappy man!

* *Montoni* Name of an Italian bandit who imprisons the heroine of *The Mysteries of Udolpho*, Catherine's favourite Gothic novel.

Gothic: form of literature popular in the eighteenth and nineteenth centuries, featuring crumbling old castles and abbeys, ghosts, death, secrets, villains, foreign settings and murder; its influence remains in modern horror stories and films.

CONTINUED ➔

Text B:

In this extract, General Tilney has told Catherine that he intends to stay up late reading pamphlets.

To be kept up for hours, after the family were in bed, by stupid pamphlets was not very likely. There must be some deeper cause: something was to be done which could be done only while the household slept; and the probability that Mrs Tilney yet lived, shut up for causes unknown, and receiving from the pitiless hands of her husband a nightly supply of coarse food, was the conclusion which necessarily followed. Shocking as was the idea, it was at least better than a death unfairly hastened, as, in the natural course of things, she must ere long be released. The suddenness of her reputed illness, the absence of her daughter, and probably of her other children, at the time – all favoured the supposition of her imprisonment. Its origin – jealousy perhaps, or wanton cruelty – was yet to be unravelled.

(a) Where does the name Tilney appear in *Atonement*?

....

(b) What similarities of subject or theme can you find in these passages, and the one prefacing *Atonement*, with McEwan's presentation of Briony in Part 1 of the novel?

....

....

....

....

....

....

....

(c) In what ways do you think Part 1 might show Gothic influences?

....

....

....

....

(d) How is the narrative style of the passages above from *Northanger Abbey*, and its effect, similar to that of Part 1 of *Atonement*?

....

....

....

....

CONTINUED ➡

Answers can be found at: www.hoddereducation.co.uk/workbookanswers

4   It is perhaps surprising to find that that *Northanger Abbey* has elements that make it a metafiction. Here is one example. Near the end of the novel, wrapping up loose strands of the plot, she refers to a young man who has married one of her characters:

> Any further definition of his merits must be unnecessary; the most charming young man in the world is instantly before the imagination of us all. Concerning the one in question, therefore, I have only to add – aware that the rules of composition forbid the introduction of a character not connected with my fable – that this was the very gentleman whose negligent servant left behind him that collection of washing-bills, resulting from a long visit at Northanger, by which my heroine was involved in one of her most alarming adventures.

(a) What is your reaction to novels that make the reader aware of the author's role, and even of the reader's own imagination, rather than remaining within the world of the fictional narrative?

....

....

(b) How might *Atonement* be influenced by this passage?

....

....

Metafiction: work that self-consciously draws attention to its status as a work of fiction and to the process of its own creation.

5   Read this passage from Charlotte Brontë's *Jane Eyre* (Chapter 26) and answer the questions that follow.

> We entered the quiet and humble temple; the priest waited in his white surplice at the lowly altar, the clerk beside him. All was still: two shadows only moved in a remote corner. My conjecture had been correct: the strangers had slipped in before us, and they now stood by the vault of the Rochesters, their backs towards us, viewing through the rails the old time-stained marble tomb, where a kneeling angel guarded the remains of Damer de Rochester, slain at Marston Moor in the time of the civil wars, and of Elizabeth, his wife.
>
> Our place was taken at the communion rails. Hearing a cautious step behind me, I glanced over my shoulder: one of the strangers – a gentleman, evidently – was advancing up the chancel. The service began. The explanation of the intent of matrimony was gone through; and then the clergyman came a step further forward, and, bending slightly towards Mr Rochester, went on.
>
> 'I require and charge you both (as ye will answer at the dreadful day of judgment, when the secrets of all hearts shall be disclosed), that if either of you know any impediment why ye may not lawfully be joined together in matrimony, ye do now confess it; for be ye well assured that so many as are coupled together otherwise than God's Word doth allow, are not joined together by God, neither is their matrimony lawful.'
>
> He paused, as the custom is. When is the pause after that sentence ever broken by reply? Not, perhaps, once in a hundred years. And the clergyman, who had not lifted his eyes from his book, and had held his breath but for a moment, was proceeding: his hand was already stretched towards Mr Rochester, as his lips unclosed to ask, 'Wilt thou have this woman for thy wedded wife?' – when a distinct and near voice said –

CONTINUED ➡

'The marriage cannot go on: I declare the existence of an impediment.'

The clergyman looked up at the speaker and stood mute; the clerk did the same; Mr Rochester moved slightly, as if an earthquake had rolled under his feet: taking a firmer footing, and not turning his head or eyes, he said, 'Proceed'.

Profound silence fell when he had uttered that word, with deep but low intonation. Presently Mr Wood said –

'I cannot proceed without some investigation into what has been asserted, and evidence of its truth or falsehood.'

'The ceremony is quite broken off,' subjoined the voice behind us. 'I am in a condition to prove my allegation: an insuperable impediment to this marriage exists.'

(a) What passage in *Atonement* does this passage from *Jane Eyre* echo, and in what ways is it similar?

....

....

....

(b) How does McEwan use intertextuality to lead the well-read reader to have particular expectations in this passage and then subvert them by not providing what is expected?

....

....

....

....

....

6 Briony is said to have read Virginia Woolf's *The Waves* three times. Read its opening, below, and answer the questions that follow.

The sun had not yet risen. The sea was indistinguishable from the sky, except that the sea was slightly creased as if a cloth had wrinkles in it. Gradually as the sky whitened a dark line lay on the horizon dividing the sea from the sky and the grey cloth became barred with thick strokes moving, one after another, beneath the surface, following each other, pursuing each other, perpetually.

As they neared the shore each bar rose, heaped itself, broke and swept a thin veil of white water across the sand. The wave paused, and then drew out again, sighing like a sleeper whose breath comes and goes unconsciously. Gradually the dark bar on the horizon became clear as if the sediment in an old wine-bottle had sunk and left the glass green.

(a) Compare the style of this passage with that of the paragraph in Part 2 of *Atonement* beginning, 'As they came out of the copse ...' (page 194).

....

....

....

....

CONTINUED ⮕

(b) Are any other parts of *Atonement* similar in style to this passage?

....

....

....

TAKING IT FURTHER

7   On a separate sheet of paper, write one or more paragraphs explaining how far you agree with this statement:

McEwan's use of intertextuality is really just 'showing off': he relies far too much on clever but obscure connections with other works.

8   *Guardian* critic Geoff Dyer writes of *Atonement's* Part 1:

Various characters come and go but the novel, at this point, seems populated mainly by its literary influences.

(*Guardian*, 22 September 2001)

(a) What do you think is implied in this statement, and how far do you agree?

....

....

....

(b) Explain how McEwan manages to surprise readers who think this.

....

....

....

9   McEwan's novel *Enduring Love* (1997) begins with a hot-air ballooning accident. Several men, including the first-person narrator, are brought together by their efforts to intervene. Subsequently, one of them develops an obsession with the narrator and stalks him, convinced that there is a bond between them. The narrator fails to convince the police or his partner that this is going on, and that he is not imagining it. In the end the stalker's actions unequivocally prove how dangerous he is. What possible similarities can you detect in theme between the two novels?

....

....

....

....

....

Challenge yourself

Find Virginia Woolf's novel *The Years* (it is online) and read some of it. What evidence can you find of it influencing Briony's style of writing?

Critical approaches

To earn credit for AO5 it is important to consider alternative interpretations of *Atonement*, including your own. One way to approach this is through looking at broad schools of criticism and at individual critics.

STARTING OUT

1   What do you see as *Atonement*'s key critical controversies? In other words, how might critics differ in their evaluation of the novel?

....

....

....

....

KEY SKILLS

Evaluating criticism

Evaluate the judgements of any critics or broad schools of criticism you cite: use them as a starting point for your own ideas.

2   *Atonement* is almost like three separate novels followed by an epilogue. Which of these statements do you agree with more?

Statement A:

> The sections into which the novel is divided make it a frustratingly disjointed work. So much seemingly vital information is missed out. The reader is forced to lurch from one world into the next, and from one character perspective to another, each time there is a section change. We are left exhausted and disappointed.

Statement B:

> The divisions of the novel reflect the utterly different worlds and perspectives of its main characters, yet in their partial overlapping demonstrate the universality of human experience. And overall, the whole novel is held together by the clever artifice of making Briony its author.

Weigh up the two views, explaining how you evaluate them.

....

....

....

....

....

....

....

....

CONTINUED ⮕

Answers can be found at: www.hoddereducation.co.uk/workbookanswers

3   How far do you think it is worthwhile or meaningful to discuss interpretations of the different characters in *Atonement* – for example, how far Robbie is in any way to blame for how he is treated, whether we should criticise both him and Cecilia for their lack of forgiveness, and even whether Briony herself is the main victim of the novel? Should we see the novel as essentially having only one character – Briony? Or do the characters merely represent McEwan's ideas about fiction? Explain your ideas.

....

....

....

....

....

....

DEVELOPING YOUR IDEAS

Be wary of making sweeping statements such as, 'Marxist criticism would see Robbie Turner as a victim of the class struggle'. It is more useful to begin with the aspects of the novel that might be of special interest to a particular school of criticism and to develop your own ideas from there.

4   Consider these broad critical approaches:
   - New historicism   ....
   - Feminist criticism   ....
   - Post-colonial criticism   ....
   - Psychoanalytical criticism   ....
   - Marxist criticism   ....

   Match each critical approach to one of these descriptions:

   A   Viewing a text as a reflection of the socio-political conditions in which it was produced, especially in terms of class and power.

   B   Sees the text as a product of its historical, social and cultural context.

   C   Sees the text as expressing repressed desires and the conflict between them and social expectations, especially shown in symbolism.

   D   Questioning evidence of patriarchal ideology and misogyny.

   E   Focuses on the presentation of ethnic minorities, especially on their exploitation.

5   Now, on the basis of your answers to Activity 4, which school of criticism might be especially interested in each of these moments in *Atonement*?

   (a) Robbie sending Cecilia the wrong version of his letter.

   ....

   (b) The fact that Robbie is convicted on the basis of Briony's evidence.

   ....

   (c) The information that the Tallis family home is now a hotel, Tilney's.

   ....

   (d) Lola's rape (or assault) and later marriage to her rapist.

   ....

   (e) The 'cameo' appearance of the minicab driver in 'London, 1999'.

   ....

CONTINUED ➡

6   Critic Hermione Lee finds *Atonement* 'impressive, engrossing, deep and surprising', with exact insights into human behaviour. She also takes the view that McEwan has managed to escape his own gender in writing as if he were a woman. Do you agree with her praise? Or does Part 2 really give a masculine view of war – McEwan's own rather than Briony's? (Note that his father was in the army.) Write a paragraph giving your views.

....

....

....

....

....

....

....

....

....

....

7   What might a critique of *Atonement* that was most interested in class struggle, capitalism, and oppression of the poor and underprivileged have to say about the following moments in the novel? Make notes on your ideas.

(a) Cecilia and Robbie struggling over the vase at the fountain.

....

....

(b) Emily reflecting on the fact that Paul Marshall has found a way to make chocolate without cocoa butter, and that he will get rich by selling this to the British army – which he does.

....

....

(c) Briony accusing Robbie of the assault; and Lola allowing the police to believe her.

....

....

(d) Grace Turner hitting the front of the police car and calling everyone liars.

....

....

(e) The corporals looking after Robbie; for example, Mace preventing him from attacking a French civilian.

....

....

CONTINUED ➡

(f) The incident when the soldiers almost kill the airman.

....

....

....

8   Read this commentary on the novel by a feminist critic and annotate it with your own responses to the
    views it presents.

Women in *Atonement* are subject to the routine patronisation and
subjection to male dominance of the 1930s and 1940s. Robbie tries
to take over from Cecilia when she is filling the vase with water,
giving her a 'command on which he tried to confer urgent
masculine authority'. Her resistance to this leads to the breaking
of the vase. When she again asserts herself by diving into the water,
the result is to turn her into a scantily clad sex object, which in turn
inspires Robbie to write her the offensive letter.

Lola is actually presented by McEwan as a sex object, who invites Paul
Marshall's attentions, and then protects him, and eventually marries
him, thus completely endorsing his sexually abusive behaviour. In other
words McEwan presents her as a sexual siren who only has herself to
blame for that happens to her, as well as to Robbie Turner.

Women in Part 2 are presented as either mad (the mother on
the farm), 'crumpet', or victims (the woman Robbie tries to save
from a German air attack). Even in Part 3, in the hospital which
could potentially be a female preserve, Sister Drummond in effect
dominates and oppresses the trainee nurses on behalf of the male
establishment, in a way which echoes the role of Aunt Lydia in
Margaret Atwood's *The Handmaid's Tale*.

Sadly, while McEwan does effectively expose some of the abuses
of women in the 1930s, as well as Briony's inherent tendency, as a
woman, to take the blame for the tragedy of the novel, he continues
to take what is essentially a male view of the events he describes.

CONTINUED ➡

TAKING IT FURTHER

9   It could be argued that McEwan abandons the suspension of disbelief in *Atonement*, presenting his novel as discourse rather than narrative. One example of this is the use of anticipation, which plucks the reader out of the narrative, as in 'Within the half hour Briony would commit her crime.' How far do you feel that his postmodern experiment still has the power to engage the reader?

....

....

> **Suspension of disbelief**: term invented by Samuel Taylor Coleridge (1772–1834) to describe the necessary acceptance of a kind of reality in a narrative by its reader in order for it to be enjoyed.

10   Use your responses to Activities 7 and 8 to write at least one paragraph about how McEwan presents oppression and victimisation in *Atonement*.

....

....

....

....

....

....

....

....

....

11   Taking into account your knowledge of other novels, write at least one paragraph on what you think is *Atonement*'s contribution to the development of the novel as a genre.

....

....

....

....

....

....

....

....

12   Read the passage below from Jane Austen's *Northanger Abbey*, in which she steps out of her narrative to call on her fellow novelists. Then answer the questions that follow.

> Let us not desert one another; we are an injured body. Although our productions have afforded more extensive and unaffected pleasure than those of any other literary corporation in the world, no species of composition has been so much decried. From

CONTINUED ➔

Answers can be found at: www.hoddereducation.co.uk/workbookanswers

pride, ignorance, or fashion, our foes are almost as many as our readers. And while the abilities of the nine-hundredth abridger of the History of England, or of the man who collects and publishes in a volume some dozen lines of Milton, Pope, and Prior, with a paper from the Spectator, and a chapter from Sterne, are eulogized by a thousand pens – there seems almost a general wish of decrying the capacity and undervaluing the labour of the novelist, and of slighting the performances which have only genius, wit, and taste to recommend them. 'I am no novel-reader – I seldom look into novels – Do not imagine that I often read novels – It is really very well for a novel.' Such is the common cant. 'And what are you reading, Miss – ?' 'Oh! It is only a novel!' replies the young lady, while she lays down her book with affected indifference, or momentary shame. 'It is only Cecilia, or Camilla, or Belinda'; or, in short, only some work in which the greatest powers of the mind are displayed, in which the most thorough knowledge of human nature, the happiest delineation of its varieties, the liveliest effusions of wit and humour, are conveyed to the world in the best-chosen language.

(a) How far could McEwan be said to be following Jane Austen's example in terms of narrative style, in her direct address to the reader?

....

....

....

....

(b) How far do you feel that *Atonement* justifies Jane Austen's view, given here, that the novel can be something worthy of serious attention, which does more than just entertain the reader? Make a bullet list to suggest what value *Atonement* has.

....

....

....

....

....

....

....

13 Consider this quotation. Robbie is optimistically contemplating his prospects:

> Now, finally, with the exercise of will, his adult life had begun. There was a story he was plotting with himself as the hero ...

What evidence is there here and elsewhere in *Atonement* for an interpretation of it as a philosophical novel, not just about fictional narrative, but about our constructing our lives by inventing and living out our personal narratives?

Plan and write an extended response to this question on a separate sheet of paper.

Challenge yourself

Think of another modern novel that you rate highly. How would you compare it with *Atonement*? Which achieves more, and how?

Boosting your skills

Whichever exam board you are studying for, you will benefit from considering all the exam-style questions in this section.

STARTING OUT

Fulfilling the Assessment Objectives

The headings in this section include the particular Assessment Objectives relevant to each subsection. In your exam response it is best to attempt to cover all the AOs by answering the question fully, rather than adding something just to cover a particular AO. However, it will help you to keep the AOs in mind in order to improve your ability to answer fully.

1 Test your knowledge of the AOs by adding its number (1–5) to the table below, which paraphrases each objective.

PARAPHRASED OBJECTIVE		NUMBER
A	Analyse how an author uses characterisation, form, language techniques and symbolism to create meaning	
B	Explore and evaluate different critical interpretations of a text, such as a Marxist interpretation, using these to inform your own	
C	Make connections between texts, for example, how two texts present and explore the theme of love, or childhood	
D	Express your own original response to texts, using relevant literary terminology and concepts, in a well-structured, coherent and fluent essay, supported by textual reference	
E	Show your understanding of contexts: the influence of the times in which a text was written, and how it is likely to be received by readers at a later date	

Preparing to answer the question (AO1)

A successful exam response starts with reading the question properly and considering how to answer it.

2 Read the following AQA (A) type question:

'In prose fiction, love always involves misunderstandings – which often have tragic consequences.'
By comparing two prose texts, explore the extent to which you agree with this statement.

(a) Underline what you think are the key words of this question.
(b) Write a numbered list of questions that arise from the statement, and that could be explored in a response.

....

....

....

....

....

....

CONTINUED ➡

Answers can be found at: www.hoddereducation.co.uk/workbookanswers

(c) In the table below, expand on four of your points insofar as they relate to *Atonement* and one other text.

POINT	ATONEMENT	OTHER TEXT
1		
2		
3		
4		

3 Consider this AQA (B) type question:

'In terms of characterisation, style and structure, McEwan invites us to approach the whole of *Atonement* as a detective novel.'

To what extent do you agree with this view? Remember to include in your answer relevant detailed exploration of McEwan's authorial methods.

On another sheet of paper, use a spider diagram or other visual method to explore ways in which the statement could be justified, and ways in which it is possible to contradict it. Use the headings 'justification' and 'contradiction' to help you organise your ideas.

CONTINUED ➡

4   Read this Edexcel style question:

Compare the ways in which the writers of your two chosen texts present the process of growing up. In your answer you must consider the following:

- **the writers' methods**
- **links between the texts**
- **the relevance of contextual factors.**

(a) For *Atonement* and one other text, make notes on six main points you could illustrate in a response, and how the two works could be linked.

POINT	ATONEMENT	OTHER TEXT
1		
2		
3		
4		
5		
6		

(b) Make notes on what contextual factors you could include in your response. Try to work comparison between the two texts into each point. Continue on a separate piece of paper.

CONTINUED ➡

Structuring your essay (AO1)

Planning is the next important stage of your response. AO1 includes the structure of your essay, and you will determine this largely at the planning stage. You should present your arguments in a logical order that leads to your conclusion.

5   The points below represent one possible rough plan for dealing with *Atonement* in a response to the question in Activity 2, repeated here for your convenience. They are not given in any particular order.

'In prose fiction, love always involves misunderstandings – which often have tragic consequences.'

By comparing two prose texts, explore the extent to which you agree with this statement.

Possible points:
- Briony misunderstands Robbie's letter.
- The tussle over the vase is a misunderstanding.
- Emily has inaccurate ideas about Paul Marshall.
- Everyone, except Cecilia and Grace, misunderstands Robbie by accusing him of rape.
- The misunderstanding over the letter actually leads to a better understanding between Cecilia and Robbie – they realise that they are in love.
- Briony completely misunderstands what she sees in the library.
- McEwan leads us to misunderstand the text, before revealing Briony as its author.

Use the space below to make a properly structured plan for this essay incorporating any of the points above and combining them with your own for *Atonement* and your chosen comparison text.

....

....

....

....

....

....

....

....

....

....

6   Now revisit your notes for the AQA (B) type question in Activity 3.

'McEwan invites us to approach the whole of *Atonement* as a detective novel, in terms of characterisation, style and structure.'

To what extent do you agree with this view? Remember to include in your answer relevant detailed exploration of McEwan's authorial methods.

Organise your points into a coherent plan for answering this question. Aim for a plan that will explore both sides of the question and then reach a conclusion that does not simply opt for one or the other.

....

....

....

....

CONTINUED ➔

....

....

....

....

....

KEY SKILLS

Explore both sides of any question or critical statement. Most questions will deliberately provide a challenge or controversy: you are unlikely to do well by simply completely agreeing or disagreeing with a statement.

---

7 Discourse markers, such as 'moreover' or 'however', make your argument easier to follow. Add suitable markers to this partial response to the question above, changing sentence punctuation where necessary, and combining simple sentences to form more fluent complex ones where appropriate. Aim for an easy flow in which the reader is led confidently from one idea to the next as the argument develops.

Ian McEwan is known to have been influenced by crime writers such as Ian Rankin. The setting of Part 1 of 'Atonement' seems to deliberately copy works by Agatha Christie. The setting is a large country house and all the characters are introduced to the reader before a crime is committed and we join a detective in trying to establish which of these characters is guilty. McEwan subverts this genre by making it clear to the reader that the accused, Robbie Turner, is not guilty. The police inspectors seem to do very little detective work, other than interviewing Briony a number of times. McEwan simply reports this as a fact rather than giving us the actual scenes in which Briony is interviewed. This removes the focus from the question of guilt. Robbie is working-class. It is a foregone conclusion that he will be suspected and accused by the upper middle-class characters around him.

There is also a sense in which the reader is made to do the detective work retrospectively. Looking back, we remember certain clues that point to Paul Marshall as the guilty party. He has a 'cruel' face, Cecilia thinks that he has touched her arm in passing, and he is identified as having 'pubic hair growing from his ears'. This gives him a hint of comic villainy. It suggests inappropriate sexuality. The scene in which he breathes heavily before telling Lola to bite the chocolate bar has sexual undertones. He is very quick to back up Lola's story about the twins scratching her.

CONTINUED ➜

Answers can be found at: www.hoddereducation.co.uk/workbookanswers

A good beginning (AO1)

8 A good essay opening will briefly show engagement with the question, may hint at what is to follow, and will quickly get into making the first major point. Consider the question below, then comment on the strengths and weaknesses of the openings that follow.

'In *Atonement*, McEwan presents Briony as a character who, at the age of 13, is old enough to take responsibility, and is therefore right to feel a lifelong need to atone for her crime.'

To what extent do you agree with this view? Remember to include in your answer relevant detailed exploration of McEwan's authorial methods.

(a)

I disagree with the stated view entirely. McEwan presents Briony as 'one of those children possessed by a desire to have the world just so', which is reflected in the careful arrangement of her model farm and dolls – a child's toys. She has a very active imagination, and gives rein to it in a childlike way. She has had very little adult supervision, her father being away much of the time, and her mother being prey to crippling migraines, so she has had little encouragement to develop an adult perspective. McEwan compares her with the more sophisticated Lola, who easily manipulates her. Briony is a victim, and the tragedy of the novel is her wasted life.

Your comment

....

....

....

....

(b)

Briony is referred to as a child, and her room, with her model farm and dolls carefully arranged, suggests that she is a child. She is easily manipulated by the more sophisticated Lola, and her childishly unbridled imagination makes her misconstrue what she sees – especially when she imagines she sees the 'sex maniac' Robbie 'attacking' Cecilia. Similarly, the scene when we see her thrashing the nettles very much presents her as a child. However, it is important to note that Briony is always presented through the authorial filter of her adult self. For the novel to give the reader a sense of resolution, we have to believe that at least to some extent the teenage Briony was old enough to commit what she later refers to as 'her crime'. Without this assumption, there would be no atonement to make, and therefore no resolution.

CONTINUED ➡

> **Your comment**
>
> ....
>
> ....
>
> ....
>
> ....

DEVELOPING YOUR IDEAS

Using textual references (AO1)

It is important to back up your argument with evidence in the form of short quotations or references to precisely identified moments in the text.

> ### KEY SKILLS
>
> If you are unsure of the wording of a quotation you want to use, do not waste valuable time searching for it: use a single key word, or refer to a passage in a way that clearly identifies it.

Where possible, embed your quotations:

Robbie, looking back, regards the study of English Literature as 'an absorbing parlour game', and rejects Leavis's view of it as being at the core of civilised life.

9   Make the points given below in your own words, embedding short quotations selected from the sections of the novel given.

(a) Emily wishes that Leon were more ambitious and could achieve more.
    Chapter 6, paragraph 2

   ....

   ....

(b) After abandoning the play, Briony feels bitterly resentful towards Lola.
    Chapter 7, paragraph 3 (nettle-slashing)

   ....

   ....

(c) Robbie regards almost any situation as preferable to being in prison.
    Page 202: new section beginning 'For a long time ...'

   ....

   ....

   ....

Your conclusion (AO1)

Even if you begin your essay well and develop your argument, it is still essential to drive this home in an effective conclusion. This should not just repeat what has already been said; nor should it introduce new points when there is no time to develop them.

CONTINUED ➡

10　Read the following conclusion to a response to the question used in Activities 2 and 5 ('In prose fiction, love always involves misunderstandings – which often have tragic consequences.' By comparing two prose texts, explore the extent to which you agree with this statement.)

In serious prose fiction, love is usually seen as something precious and worth struggling for, and this is certainly the case both in 'Jane Eyre' and 'Atonement'. Jane struggles for the love of Rochester, and suffers the pain of losing him at the altar due to the 'misunderstanding' of his attempted bigamy. The pair only regain each other after further suffering, and after Rochester is, in effect, punished for his sins by the loss of his sight. In 'Atonement', there is no such happy ending, except in Briony's imagination, as portrayed in Part 3. Since the lovers both die due to the violence of war, it can be said that the central misunderstanding of the novel has had truly tragic consequences.

What strengths does this conclusion have? Try to list at least three.

....

....

....

....

11　Write an effective conclusion to this essay based on a comparison between *Atonement* and another novel of your choice.

....

....

....

....

....

....

....

....

....

....

KEY SKILLS

Be concise

Aim to write concisely. Waffling will only suggest to the examiner that you are unclear about what you want to say. Do not begin your conclusion with a phrase such as: 'As I believe I have demonstrated throughout this essay ...'.

Close analysis of the text (AO2)

12 You will not be given a passage-based question, but you will probably be allowed to take an unmarked copy of the text into the exam with you. If you are writing about *Atonement* for coursework, you will have even more opportunity to find relevant quotations and analyse their language.

When commenting on style and language, you will find it more effective to concentrate on a few passages and make detailed comments than to generalise about McEwan's style throughout the novel.

Practise this by writing at least one paragraph analysing how McEwan's style and language show Robbie's state of mind in the two final paragraphs of Part 2 (pages 264–5).

....

....

....

....

....

....

....

....

....

....

....

....

....

....

13 Try to weave your analysis into sentences containing your quotations.
Add analysis in the gaps in the following paragraph.

Early on in Part 2, Robbie has the ....

to rephrase Nettle's .... comments

on 'Frog crumpet'. However, as his wound and tiredness take their toll he loses

...., and begins to attack a French

motorist who has sounded his horn because Robbie is in his way.

14 Reread the final three paragraphs of the novel. Then on a separate sheet of paper write a fluent paragraph evaluating Briony's mental and emotional state at this point, and giving your views on how far this provides a satisfying sense of catharsis.

Catharsis: term from ancient Greek tragedy referring to the sense of emotional calm and resolution with which a drama (or in this case a novel) should leave its audience.

CONTINUED ➡

Using context (AO3)

You will be expected to show knowledge of relevant context. Remember that this includes:

- possible social and historical influences on the author at the time of writing
- the social conditions at the times in which the novel is set – mostly the 1930s and Britain during World War II, and how the author interprets them
- literary influences on the author – including in McEwan's case the whole history of the novel as a genre
- influences on the audience's reception of the text.

The important thing is to make sure it really is relevant, and not just 'bolted on' to your argument for the sake of it.

15 Read these two extracts from student essays on the role of women in two novels, including *Atonement*. Annotate what you think are their good and bad points. Which do you think uses context more effectively? Write an 'examiner' comment beneath each one.

Text A:

> Lola is an ambiguous character, who in part represents male ambivalence about women in the 1930s. Two years older than the intelligent but socially naïve Briony, Lola manipulates her cousin into giving her the lead part in the play, even though she would rather not be in the play at all. She also lies to Paul Marshall, saying that she has been to see 'Hamlet' to try to impress him, and claiming to Briony that the twins have been giving her 'Chinese burns', when in fact she has been hurt by Paul Marshall. Later she covers for him, claiming again that her scratches are from them, and allowing him, as her rapist, to go free while Robbie is imprisoned. Women in the 1930s were expected to satisfy men's wishes and bow to their superior judgement. Lola therefore puts loyalty to Marshall before any sense of sisterhood towards Briony.

Your comment:

....

....

....

....

....

....

CONTINUED ➡

Text B:

McEwan presents women in a number of ways. Cecilia is initially rather lazy and spoilt, which as the daughter of wealthy parents she can afford to be, but she also has the independence of spirit that women in Britain had increasingly developed since the First World War. Emily reflects the attitudes of the older generation and her class in regarding women's education as 'at best an innocent lark', and hopes Cecilia will find a wealthy husband. Lola, meanwhile, is led by the sexual politics of the 1930s, as well as her willingness to be flattered by male attention, to betray Briony and lie to protect Paul Marshall. It could also be argued that at the time she might have feared being blamed herself. However, McEwan gives us little reason to sympathise with her; the narrative is never told from her viewpoint, and she eventually marries her rapist. A recent reader, in the wake of the 'Me Too' campaign, might be more inclined to see her as a victim of sexual abuse.

Your comment:

....

....

....

....

....

....

16 Write a paragraph about the portrayal of social class in Part 2 of the novel, weaving appropriate context into your comments.

....

....

....

....

....

CONTINUED ➡

Answers can be found at: www.hoddereducation.co.uk/workbookanswers

....

....

....

....

Exploring connections across texts (AO4)

Depending on your syllabus, you may be asked to compare *Atonement* with another text. For example, you may be asked to compare the way in which authors present an aspect of love, or childhood. Even if your exam does not ask for comparison, this is still a useful exercise to develop your ideas about *Atonement* and how it fits into the genre of the novel.

17 Use the table below to make notes comparing *Atonement* with another text of your choice in any categories that are relevant.

HOW THEY PRESENT ...	ATONEMENT	OTHER TEXT
A The relative roles of men and women		
B Romantic love		
C Childhood and/or growing up		
D Social class		
E Conflict		

CONTINUED ➡

18 One way in which *Atonement* is unusual is its narrative structure, including its overall framing device and its use of viewpoint. How does this compare with one other novel that you know, and which do you find more successful? Explain your ideas.

....

....

....

....

....

....

Interpretations (AO5)

19 One way to develop your own interpretation of the novel is to consider those of critics. Academic Brian Finney, in a long essay on *Atonement*, available online, 'Briony's Stand Against Oblivion', argues that the self-conscious metafictional framework of *Atonement* represents the human experience, and even the uncertain nature of reality:

> To draw attention to the narrative process is not an act of self indulgence on the part of the metafictional novelist, as suggested by a few of this book's reviewers. It is central to the book's concerns. In the first place when novelists force us to understand the constructed nature of their characters they invite us simultaneously to reflect on the way subjectivity is similarly constructed in the non-fictional world we inhabit.

How far do you agree with this view of *Atonement*?

....

....

....

....

....

....

20 In some of his novels, for example, *Saturday*, McEwan links social and political events to the personal. Brian Finney comments on *Atonement*:

> Briony teeters at the brink of adolescence, just as Lola 'longed to throw off the last restraints of childhood'. The novel invites us to see these two girls as symptomatic of the state of Britain and the West at this period of history.

How far do you agree? Could it even be argued that McEwan is more concerned with the large-scale political and social picture than with individuals?

....

....

....

....

....

....

CONTINUED ➔

21 McEwan makes extensive use of intertextuality, alluding to numerous other texts. Do you think it is possible to appreciate *Atonement* only if one understands these references?

....

....

....

....

TAKING IT FURTHER

22 Go back and review your responses to Activities 2 (developed in Activity 5), 3 (developed in Activities 6 and 7), 4 and 8. Choose one of the questions explored in these activities and write a full exam-style response to it below. Continue on a separate sheet of paper.

....

....

....

....

....

....

....

....

....

23 Reread Activity 1 to remind yourself of the AOs. Then reread your response to Activity 22 and see if you think you have fulfilled them all. Consider the checklist below:

- Is there a clear introduction that engages with the question straight away and anticipates your intended line of argument?

- Does the structure of your response lead the reader in a logical way through your argument?

- Have you explored the question rather than simply asserting one viewpoint and not considering others?

- Have you included relevant context?

- Does your writing flow easily with ideas linked by connectives that point to where your argument is going, such as 'However' or 'On the other hand'?

- Have you backed up your ideas with evidence in the form of short quotations or precise references to moments in the text?

- Does your conclusion draw your response to a close without simply repeating yourself, or introducing any last-minute ideas that you have no time to develop?

Challenge yourself

Frank Kermode, in the *London Review of Books*, calls *Atonement* a philosophical novel, and suggests that 'The pleasure it gives depends as much on our suspending belief as on our suspending disbelief.' What do you think he means, and do you agree? You can read the whole review by searching for the novel title and the quoted sentence.

Answers can be found at: www.hoddereducation.co.uk/workbookanswers

The publisher would like to thank the following for permission to reproduce copyright material:

Acknowledgments:

Throughout: Ian McEwan: from *Atonement* (Jonathan Cape 2001), reprinted by permission of The Random House Group Limited © 2001; **p.58: Virginia Woolf:** from *Mrs Dalloway* (Random House, 1925), public domain; **pp.61–62:** from 'The Defence of Dunkirk' (*The Times*, 30 May 1940), public domain; **pp.62–63:** from 'Waiting to embark' (*The Times*, 5 June 1940), public domain; **p.63:** from 'Rapid flow of troops through Dunkirk' (*The Times*, 1 June 1940), public domain; **p.64:** from 'Names wiped out' (*The Times*, 7 June 1940), public domain; **p.67, 68, 69, 76–77: Jane Austen:** from *Northanger Abbey* (R. Bentley, 1817), public domain; **pp.69–70: Charlotte Brontë:** from *Jane Eyre* (W.W. Norton and Company, 1847), public domain; **p.70: Virginia Woolf:** from *The Waves* (Random House, 1931), public domain; **p.71: Geoff Dyer:** from 'Who's afraid of influence?' (*Guardian*, 22 September 2001), reproduced under fair use; **p.90: Brian Finney:** from 'Briony's stand against oblivion: The marking of fiction in Ian McEwan's Atonement', *Journal of Modern Literature*, 3, pp.68–82 (Indiana University Press, 2004), republished with permission of Indiana University Press, permission conveyed through Copyright Clearance Center, Inc.; **p.91: Frank Kermode:** from 'Point of view', *London Review of Books*, 23(19), pp.8–9 (4 October 2001), reproduced under fair use.

Every effort has been made to trace all copyright holders, but if any have been inadvertently overlooked, the Publishers will be pleased to make the necessary arrangements at the first opportunity.

Although every effort has been made to ensure that website addresses are correct at time of going to press, Hodder Education cannot be held responsible for the content of any website mentioned. It is sometimes possible to find a relocated web page by typing in the address of the home page for a website in the URL window of your browser.

Orders: please contact Bookpoint Ltd, 130 Milton Park, Abingdon, Oxon OX14 4SB. Telephone: (44) 01235 827720. Fax: (44) 01235 400401. Lines are open 9.00–17.00, Monday to Saturday, with a 24-hour message answering service. Visit our website at www.hoddereducation.co.uk

ISBN 9781510434929

© Steve Eddy 2018

First published in 2018 by
Hodder Education
An Hachette UK Company,
Carmelite House, 50 Victoria Embankment
London EC4Y 0DZ

Impression number   5 4 3 2 1

Year 2022 2021 2020 2019 2018

Cover photo © abzee/istockphoto.com

Illustrations by Integra Software Services Pvt. Ltd., Pondicherry

Typeset by Integra Software Services Pvt. Ltd., Pondicherry, India

Printed in Dubai

A catalogue record for this title is available from the British Library.

HODDER EDUCATION

t: 01235 827827
e: education@bookpoint.co.uk
w: hoddereducation.co.uk

ISBN 978-1-5104-3492-9